# The Simple Stress Solution

Your key to be free

Copyright © 2017 Vern & Calista Ward

Cover design & illustrations © 2017 Jadon Ward

Formatting and layout by Ethan Larsen

All rights reserved. No portion of this book may be reproduced, stored in a retrieval system, or transmitted in any form or media or by any means, electronic, mechanical, photocopying, recording, or otherwise, without the prior written permission of the publisher. If you would like to use material from the book (other than for review purposes), prior written permission must be obtained by contacting the publisher at info@okanaganpublishinghouse.ca.

Published by:

## Okanagan Publishing House
1024 Lone Pine Crt
Kelowna, BC V1P 1M7
www.okanaganpublishinghouse.ca

Printed in the United States of America

3rd Edition, February 2018

10   9   8   7   6   5   4   3

ISBN: 978-0-9938627-4-8

# The Simple Stress Solution

## Your key to be free

**DR. CALISTA & VERN WARD**

OKANAGAN
PUBLISHING HOUSE

# ACKNOWLEDGEMENTS

Dr. Calista and Vern Ward would like to acknowledge the efforts of those who contributed to this project.

Vern would like to be the first to highlight the patience, support and assistance of Calista in helping wade through many revisions of this manuscript, honing and clarifying the ideas that were revealed to him as he spent thousands of hours working with clients. He also would like to thank his children for putting up with endless lectures on the principles and how they apply to their lives. Clearly no other form of punishment could ever be more effective than that!

Calista would like to acknowledge that despite Vern's many attempts to put in writing the principles he utilizes every day, this workbook would not have gone beyond the idea stage were it not for the relentless efforts of their oldest son, Jadon Ward, who believed in the project and the concepts enough to guide them into this workbook format. Jadon was specifically involved in editing and overseeing publication, while Ethan Larsen assisted in formatting the manuscript.

Finally, an important acknowledgement of the true Source of the principles that provide a solution to the stress we experience. May we all seek to continually align ourselves with this Source.

# TABLE OF CONTENTS

| | |
|---|---|
| Preface | 1 |
| Day 1: Introduction & Welcome | 3 |
| **PART 1: IDENTIFYING STRESS** | **9** |
| Day 2: Identifying Stress Overview | 11 |
| Day 3: What Is Stress? | 15 |
| Day 4: What Is Your Stress? | 21 |
| Day 5: How Does Your Stress Affect You? | 27 |
| Day 6: Personal Stress Profile | 37 |
| **PART 2: UNDERSTANDING STRESS** | **41** |
| Day 7: What's Behind Stress?: Emotions | 43 |
| Day 8: What's Behind Stress?: Desires | 47 |
| Day 9: What's Behind Stress?: Reactions | 57 |
| Day 10: What Is The Stress Spiral?: Stuck | 63 |
| Day 11: What Is The Stress Spiral?: Extinguish | 67 |
| Day 12: What Is The Stress Spiral?: Express | 73 |
| Day 13: What Is The Stress Spiral?: Escape | 79 |
| Day 14: What Can We Use To Get Our Of It?: Part 1 | 91 |
| Day 15: What Can We Use To Get Our Of It?: Part 2 | 97 |
| Day 16: Understanding Stress Review | 101 |
| **PART 3: REDUCING STRESS** | **103** |
| Day 17: Why Do We Need A Stress Regulator? | 105 |
| Day 18: Stress + Performance | 107 |
| Day 19: Stress Capacity | 113 |
| Day 20: What Is The Stress Cycle?: Origins | 125 |
| Day 21: What Is The Stress Cycle?: Vending Machine | 133 |
| Day 22: What Is The Stress Cycle?: De-Stress Cycle | 137 |
| Day 23: Regulating Stress: Missing Link | 143 |
| Day 24: Regulating Stress: Stress Neutralizer | 149 |
| Day 25: Regulating Stress: Mountain Climber | 155 |
| Day 26: Regulating Stress: Hot Shower | 159 |
| Day 27: Regulating Stress: The Utility of Humility | 167 |
| Day 28: Regulating Stress: The Dashboard Of Life | 171 |
| Day 29: Summary + Next Steps | 177 |
| Day 30: What Now? Join Us! | 181 |

# PREFACE

If you're reading this, it's because you're interested in finding out how to deal with stress. Perhaps your life has become unmanageable, you are feeling overwhelmed, and your body is shutting down. Maybe you are escaping in unhealthy ways, and you know you need to change. It could be that you are taking out your stress on others, or it is impacting your work and relationships.

Stress affects everyone who is alive, and there are many stress management programs out there. These programs tend to focus on ways to handle the symptoms of stress. However, there is a surprising lack of information available that addresses the underlying root of stress. Therefore, the attempts that we make to just manage stress will always leave us fighting it again, day after day.

We hope that you will use this information which follows as a way to look at stress differently; to embrace the positive aspects, and eliminate the negative effects. In this process of self-discovery, we believe that you will become better equipped to manage the stressful feelings you may have. It will also assist you in dealing with other negative emotions that are associated with stress. Finally, it will help you address the resulting behaviors and addictions that can sometimes interfere with our lives when we aren't coping well with stress.

In short, this workbook is intended to assist you in identifying, understanding, and reducing your stress. In order to do that, you will be invited to participate in a journey that will lead you out of the place where you may be 'stuck' feeling 'stressed out' (the swamp), to a destination where you will be better equipped to handle what life throws at you. Is it possible to eliminate stress entirely from your life? No. Is there a way to instantly regulate it so that you can calmly and efficiently make a plan to move forward without feeling overwhelmed? Yes. That's what you will be learning through this process.

You could be reading this out of curiosity, as part of the companion online course, or as a follow up to an in-person session. In any case, this will workbook will provide you a chance to engage with the material, and start asking questions that will further relate the ideas to your own life. This process will only be as effective as you make it. Being honest with yourself may be difficult at times, but it is necessary if you want to get out of the 'swamp.'

This workbook is designed to give you sections that you can read every day within a five minute timeframe, plus the time that you spend answering the questions associated with each day. It can be spread out over the full 30 day timeframe for maximum benefit, but if you want to proceed at a faster pace, that is entirely up to you – the entire workbook can be read in approximately 2 hours. You can go back later and answer the questions later if you choose. Either way, let's begin!

# INTRODUCTION

## DAY 1: WELCOME

### INTRODUCTION

Welcome to the workbook! We're excited that you've decided to take a positive step to deal with your stress, and hope that you will learn what you are looking for. We've designed this workbook to follow along the process that thousands of our clients have used to find relief from the stress they were feeling in their lives. The sections in the workbook correspond to the lectures in the Simple Stress Solution online course, which you can access by signing up at: **thestresscenter.ca**.

First, you'll be spending time learning about the basics of stress. Then, through the workbook questions, you'll take these principles you are about to learn and apply them to your world. Your life will be profoundly changed as a result!

### CHALLENGE TO BE SKEPTICAL

Now, if you aren't ready to believe us, we say, "PERFECT!" If that means you are skeptical of everything you are reading as a result, that's fine. Really. Being skeptical is good, in our opinion, because it means that you will be challenging everything we have to say. Why would we want that? Because it means that you will be doing three things:

  1. *Paying attention to the concepts*

  2. *Relating them to your experience*

*3. Judging them to be either false and useless,*

*or true and relevant*

If you do these three things and it turns out that what we are saying is true, you will apply them to your life and have less stress. That is our goal - to help you find a healthier, less stressed way of living. And because we know these simple principles are powerful and DO WORK, we are excited about starting this process with you.

---

**Key Concept:** *"Being skeptical is good, in our opinion, because it means that you will be challenging everything we have to say."*

---

When we are done you will have a simple, powerful process that you can access to keep your life stress free. You will be able to access it in minutes - and it will work! That's the good news.

The bad news is that you need to understand the ideas behind the three step process for it to work. That will take a little patience on your part, but we promise, if you stay with us, it will be worth it. These principles have been proven. How can you trust us? Ironically, not only because we are both professionals with advanced degrees and years of experience as therapists helping people who are stressed. You should trust us because we've actually developed and tested out these principles in real life!

## WE'VE BEEN STRESSED

We want to let you know that we know what you're going through. At least the stress part. We have five biological children and twin babies that we are adopting who are very active toddlers. Do we need to say any more, really? They are amazing kids, and we love them more than anything, but having lots of children is not the recipe for how to 'De-stress Yourself!'

We've been through difficult circumstances, too. Starting to have kids when you're young and going to school, and not having enough time or money for them because you're dealing with health concerns, lawsuits, a near bankruptcy, a fire, moving, career changes and marriage crises – all at the same time! – do not tend to be part of what professionals recommend to reduce stress.

But here's the good news. We not only survived the crazy stress of our lives the past twenty four years, but we have emerged on the other side with having learned the principles of how you can too. Stress is never easy to endure, but it is a part of life. The sooner we have tools and strategies to reduce and eliminate stress, the faster we can get on with enjoying our lives again. Here we go!

## WORKBOOK OVERVIEW

Let's take a look at the big picture first of all. This course is split into sections designed to help you with three things:

1. *Identifying your stress* – although you might think that it's easy to identify your stress and how it affects you, chances are there are things that you might not realize about the impact of stress on

your life, and what things are the most frequent causes of stress in your life.

2. **Understanding your stress** – everyone's stress is different, but all stress is created in the same way. Understanding the dynamics of your stress is essential if we want to deal with the core issues creating it!

3. **Reducing your stress** – this is the 'good' part! Finding out exactly how to reduce or eliminate your experience of stress is what you're after if you're reading this right now. We can guarantee that if you follow this process, it will happen!

Throughout this workbook, you will be exploring these in more depth, and getting answers to the questions that go along with each section.

# DAY 1 WORKSHEET

## REACT

1. Do you honestly believe that there could be a simple solution that would enable you to deal with stress in your life? If not, then you're naturally going to be skeptical – which is a good thing!

## REFLECT

1. What was the most stressful time that you experienced in your life?

2. Think back to what was going on at the time, and the areas of your life that were impacted. List them below.

3. How did you manage to get through that time in your life (if it isn't what you're going through right now)? Did you manage to actually solve the underlying issue, or just deal with symptoms?

4. Describe what it would look like for you to be free of stress. What would be different and what would you notice first?

5. How long have you been living with too much stress?

6. Describe the last time that you spent more than a month (not including vacation!) feeling stress-free.

7. How do you think that it is possible to get to that place again?

## RESPOND

1. Make a note of the questions that you have as you progress through the workbook. See whether these doubts and fears that may exist right now get addressed by the end of the book. Feel free to contact the authors if there are still unanswered questions that you would like to find out more about by emailing **info@thestresscenter.ca**

# Part 1:
# IDENTIFYING STRESS

# DAY 2: IDENTIFYING STRESS OVERVIEW

(Complete worksheet prior to Day 2 reading)

## *REACT*

1. What are the first images that pop into your mind when you hear the word stress?

## *REFLECT*

1. What are the things that have routinely caused you stress throughout your life?

2. What do you see as a common theme among those stress causing items? (i.e. workplace, financial, relationships, parenting, etc.)

## *RESPOND*

1. As you continue through this process, be open to learning about other ways of looking at what stress is, and how it affects you, that may be different from what you're used to. Take note of these in a notebook or journal to document what you may be discovering.

# DAY 2: SECTION 1 OVERVIEW

## OUTLINE OF SECTION

We begin by asking three questions:

1. What is stress?

2. What is your stress?

3. How does your stress affect you?

Let's look at each of these in turn, and expand a little so you understand exactly why we are wanting to answer these questions.

## WHAT IS STRESS?

Although this seems like an obvious question, it is not actually that easy to answer. We all have ideas as to what stress means, and how we define stress influences how we attempt to reduce it. We will look briefly at our preconceptions of stress, some background and science around stress research, and then come up with an easy to understand definition that we will be using throughout the course.

## WHAT IS YOUR STRESS?

Here is where we look at your own life and the things that you think tend to increase your own stress level. For some people, it is workplace stress – demands your boss places on you, or conflict with co-workers. For others, it is when they get home that the stress begins. Issues like relationship conflict with a spouse or children, the financial stress involving how to make ends meet, or the burden of caring for a loved one who is ill while trying to find time for yourself, are all things that create stress for individuals. Discovering your own stress triggers can help you build a plan to manage these areas of your life.

## HOW DOES YOUR STRESS AFFECT YOU?

Regardless of where our stress comes from, we all handle it differently. For some people, it affects their mood – they are irritable or anxious. Others increase the amount they smoke as a way to cope with stress – what they do is affected the most. Others can be affected socially as they withdraw from engaging with friends and their support network. Stress can also affect us physically, for instance, when we start getting migraines or our back muscles start cramping up. Finally, stress can affect our memory, or our ability to focus and concentrate, which in turn can increase our stress level.

---

**Key Concept:** *"Regardless of where our stress comes from, we all handle it differently."*

---

Once these questions have been answered, and you have determined your own 'stress-profile' it is possible to move to the next sections – understanding what is behind the patterns of stress that we have developed, and developing effective ways to reduce or eliminate our experience of stress.

# DAY 3: "WHAT IS STRESS?"

## IMAGES OF STRESS

Let's begin by taking a look at what we mean by stress. Take a moment now to write down some things that you feel might be adding to your stress. Here are some examples to get you thinking...

1. Your boss announcing that you have to finish the project by end of the day, a task that seems pretty much impossible, but he's in a bad mood so you don't dare challenge him/her.

2. You look at your bank balance and see that there's not enough money left to get you through the rest of the month.

3. The tension you might feel in the pit of your stomach when you imagine how the argument with your spouse will go tonight when you get home.

4. Imagining the battle with your kids at supper when you're trying to get your kids to eat their vegetables!

We all think of different things when we hear the word stress. Typically, stress doesn't normally conjure up happy thoughts or feelings. It's most often experienced as a negative emotion – something we're going to help you reduce.

## DEFINING STRESS

Okay – so our first task is to identify stress. Although it may seem obvious to us what stress is, it's actually difficult to define. In fact, there isn't one particular definition of stress that is universally accepted. The father of stress research himself, Dr. Hans Selye, added to this confusion by saying: "Stress, in addition to being itself, was also the cause of itself, and the result of itself." We use the word stress to refer to a number of things, and that's why we need to sort it out.

## EXAMPLE OF TASHA

Let's use an example to provide some insight:

Tasha is just about to leave work to go home when her boss walks by her, and causally drops a file on her desk. "Make sure this is done by 8:00 am tomorrow – the client is coming by the office to review it at 8:30." Tasha instantly realizes her carefully laid plans to celebrate her daughter's birthday this evening with her family would have to change, or she would risk disappointing her boss. She also feels a knot in the pit of her stomach as she realizes the painful conversation that will involve her husband and kids as they realize they won't be able to go out as planned. She feels her heart rate rise and senses her breathing rate increasing. As she collects her papers and the file and walks to the car she realizes that she forgot her phone inside her office along with her keys. Her frustration mounts as she bangs on the door to get back into the office, but the receptionist has already left for the day. She can't get a hold of her family to let them know that not only will she not be able to meet them at the restaurant for supper, but that she will be late getting back now too. She feels her stress level rising inside of her and she pulls a cigarette out of her purse and lights it up. Her muscles tighten in her neck as she strains to see if anyone else is coming out of the office. Slowly she slumps down against the front door and a tear comes to her eye. Most people might say that Tasha is now officially stressed!

---

**Key Concept:** *"Stress, in addition to being itself, was the cause of itself, and the result of itself". - Dr. Hans Seyle*

---

Let's go back now and analyze what's going on so we can discover more about stress and how it works. To begin with, Tasha has a demand placed on her (desk – literally!) by her boss. Her response to that demand determines what happens next. Due to her accurate perception that she won't be able to do what she had planned AND get the file ready for tomorrow, she is feeling pressure – both to not disappoint her boss (on whose opinion her job depends!) and pressure not to disappoint her family (who are looking forward to spending the evening with her). She and her body respond to this pressure in a variety of ways. Physically she starts feeling symptoms that are part of the release of the stress hormones cortisol and adrenaline. Heart and breathing rate increase and her stomach feels queasy. Her muscles tighten and she gets a knot in her neck. Mentally her mind is clouded by the stress hormones, and she becomes forgetful, leaving her phone and keys in the office. Behaviorally she responds by lighting a cigarette as a coping mechanism to alleviate stress. Finally she is affected emotionally, and starts to cry silently due to the situation in which she finds herself.

What's going on?

## SUMMARY OF BASICS

So the basics are as follows:

1. We encounter events/pressures in life.

2. These are called 'stressors' because our bodies respond to them by elevating our levels of stress or physiological arousal.

3. This state of stress, if it is too much for us to handle or if it lasts too long, ends up in us getting 'stressed out' - a feeling of being overwhelmed with symptoms which don't go away.

## BACKGROUND

When humans were living in a world where they could be attacked by sabre-toothed tigers and would need all of their energy mobilized instantly – the 'fight or flight' response – this physiological activation was not only helpful, but necessary for survival. Unfortunately, our bodies are like a light switch, and when we feel threatened in other ways, our brains still hit the 'on' button and we experience symptoms of activation. In our modern world, with the fast pace of life, and ever-increasing demands to do more and be more, we can stay in this heightened state of arousal for longer periods of time – some people never seem to leave it!

Over time though, living in this state of being 'stressed out' exhausts our bodies and our immune system suffers, setting us up for the onset of serious illness or other conditions that will compromise body functions. According to the American Institute of Stress, 75-90% of all doctor's office visits are for stress-related ailments and complaints!

## STRESS DEFINITION

So the definition of stress could come down to a very basic idea – "Our response to demands (stressors) placed on us." We will expand and clarify that further as we go, but the important thing to recognize is that our responses are going to be varied depending on the type of stressor, and the type of person we are, which determines how it affects us.

---

**Key Concept:** *Stress is: "Our response to demands (stressors) placed upon us."*

---

# DAY 3 WORKSHEET

## *REACT*

1. What is your reaction to the definition? How might it be too simplistic?

## *REFLECT*

1. Based on this definition of stress, what are the demands that are being placed on you that are creating stress?

2. What do you think your typical responses are to these demands?

## *RESPOND*

1. Today, make a note of the times when demands are placed on you and your reactions to them.

# DAY 4: WHAT IS YOUR STRESS?

## TYPES OF STRESSORS

Let's look first at the types of demands or stressors. There are three main types of demands that differ in severity. We will start with the most significant ones first.

1. **CATASTROPHES**. The first type are, fortunately, not common. These types of stressors are ones which are likely featured on CNN. 'Acts of God' fit into this category – events like, floods, hurricanes or tornados, fires, etc. The aftereffects of these large scale disasters frequently produce great amounts of stress and negative health repercussions.

2. **SIGNIFICANT LIFE CHANGES** refer to those events which may be typically expected to happen along the way in someone's life, but which are nonetheless difficult to handle and adjust to. These include things like the death of a spouse, a divorce, a loss of a job, etc. Exposure to these can increase vulnerability to physical illnesses.

3. **DAILY HASSLES** are low level happenings that everyone faces on an ongoing basis. These would include things like rush hour traffic, long lineups, annoying co-workers or housemates, etc. An accumulation of everyday hassles can lead to high levels of stress.

**Key Concept:** *"There are three main categories of stressors or demands: Catastrophes, Significant Life Changes, and Daily Hassles."*

## DAILY HASSLES IN DEPTH

It is the last category of everyday stressors that we are going to pay attention to, as this category consists of what are, by far, the most common sources of stress. For most of us who are busy, the demands of our lives just seem to accumulate and we aren't aware of how we are being affected. We also don't take the time to sort out what categories of stressors affect us the most. The following is a list of sub-categories of daily hassles that may be affecting you. Fill in the blanks with an example that may be more relevant to you.

1. **VOCATIONAL** (Workplace)

    1. Workload management

    2. Co-worker relationships

    3. Conflict with boss

    4. Other_____

2. **MARITAL** (Marriage/Relationships)

    1. Communication

    2. Roles/Responsibilities

    3. Connection/Intimacy

    4. Other_____

### 3. PARENTAL (Parenting)

1. Discipline structure
2. Sibling conflict
3. Attitude/Independence
4. Other_____

### 4. FINANCIAL

1. Debt overwhelm
2. Over-spending
3. Shopping addiction
4. Other_____

### 5. PHYSIOLOGICAL

1. Illness
2. Pain
3. Stress-related conditions
4. Other_____

### 6. EMOTIONAL

1. Coping with toxic emotions
2. Managing mood swings
3. Feeling 'at the edge'
4. Other_____

### 7. SPIRITUAL

    1. Feeling 'disconnected' from God

    2. Doubts/fears re: faith

    3. Spiritual 'abuse'

    4. Other_____

## THEY ALL TAKE THEIR TOLL

Regardless of what types of demands or stressors you are facing, or how severe they may be, they will all take a certain toll on you. We normally think of stressors as being bad, but that may not actually be the case. Demands can be positive or negative and still create stress. Even positive experiences may take time and energy away from us and spread us thin. Nailing a presentation at work is a good thing, but it may mean that we have had to devote a lot of energy preparing for it, and are exhausted once it's over.

Trying to rate the impact of various stressors was something the Holmes-Rahe Stress Scale attempts to do. It took a collection of routine life events and rated them according to how much stress they created in the individual. The highest rating of 100 points was reserved for the Death of a Spouse. Other events were still significant, but lower. Fired at Work was worth 47 points, for instance. Christmas was only 12 points, but it still was on the list.

What the researchers found was interesting. For those who had experienced a significant number of stressful life events in the past year, such that their total was over 300 points, there was a 90%

chance that they would experience a major illness. That sounds pretty serious!

We thought so too when we started evaluating our own lives during our first five years of marriage. Although we knew our lives had been stressful, we didn't realize that our average score for those years did not go below 400! We managed to not succumb to a significant illness, but those years did take their toll on us. We also became aware that stress affected each of us differently and that our awareness of the impact that stress was having was a key part of helping us understand and manage it better. That is where we now turn.

**Want to take the Holmes & Rahe Stress Scale?**

**Email info@thestresscenter.ca to get a copy today!**

# DAY 4 WORKSHEET

## *REACT*

1. Were you aware of these different areas that can create stress? How surprising is it?

## *REFLECT*

1. Based on this definition of stress, what are the demands that are being placed on you that are creating stress?

2. What do you think your typical responses are to these demands?

## *RESPOND*

1. Today, make a note of the times when demands are placed on you and your reactions to them.

# DAY 5: HOW DOES YOUR STRESS AFFECT YOU?

## AREAS OF LIFE AFFECTED BY STRESS

Let's identify four primary areas of our lives which are affected the most by stress:

1. Physical

2. Emotional

3. Behavioral

4. Mental

Now we're going to examine each of these in turn to help familiarize you with the symptoms of stress related to each.

## PHYSICAL SYMPTOMS OF STRESS

Many of us don't realize that the symptoms of stress most commonly felt are those which affect our bodies. When we are stressed and stress hormones like cortisol and adrenaline flow through us at levels that prepare us for action, our bodies are affected. Over time, the effects of these stress hormones create symptoms which negatively impact our functioning. Learning how to identify when these symptoms are present is a huge first step to identifying a need to address our stress and make changes. Check out the list which follows to identify your primary physical symptoms of stress:

__Headaches

__Indigestion

__Stomach aches

__Sweaty palms

__Dizziness

__Nausea

__Back, Neck, Shoulder, or other muscle tightness or pain

__Jaw pain, possibly from clenching your teeth

__Racing heart

__Restlessness

__Tiredness

__Sleep problems (can't get to sleep, interrupted sleep, or early awakening)

__Nightmares

## EMOTIONAL SYMPTOMS OF STRESS

Another key area affected by stress is our emotional health and well-being. Just like Tasha in the story, she started feeling like she was on the brink of crying even though that wouldn't necessarily have been a productive way to manage the situation. Why do we sometimes get to the point where we aren't able to better handle what's going on inside of us emotionally? Our ability to cope and deal with emotions is directly linked to the level of stress we have to endure, as stress zaps our energy and resources. Here are some examples of symptoms that may be familiar to you.

__Nervousness or anxiety

___Tearfulness, or feeling like you are on the brink of crying

___Edginess, or feeling like you are ready to snap at others or explode

___Feeling powerless or helpless

___Feeling under pressure

___Loneliness

___Having a "hair trigger" or getting upset very quickly or easily

___Feeling unhappy and not being able to identify why

___Feeling chronic annoyance

___Feeling chronic boredom

___Feeling like nothing is important or meaningful

___Feeling "flat" and no longer taking pleasure in things

___Feeling distant from everyone, like you're behind a glass wall.

## BEHAVIOURAL SYMPTOMS OF STRESS

When we see a change in our actions because of an increase in stress, it's usually not positive. Although a certain amount of stress may increase our motivation to complete a project, or start an exercise program, high levels of stress produce in us responses that usually interfere with our ability to function, or at least are detrimental in some way. In the example above, Tasha resorts to lighting a cigarette as a way of trying to relax because she is stressed. Taking out our stress on others by becoming irritable or critical can also interfere with relationships and, ironically, increase stress as well. Here is a list of some common behavioral symptoms that can accompany high levels of stress. Check off those which may affect you.

\_\_Drinking more or too much

\_\_Using any other drugs to "self medicate" stress or make you feel "ok"

\_\_Compulsive eating or eating to change your mood

\_\_Grinding your teeth

\_\_Smoking more or compulsively

\_\_Bossing others around

\_\_Arguing with others or picking fights

\_\_Criticizing others

\_\_Not getting daily tasks at home or work completed

\_\_Sleeping too much

## MENTAL SYMPTOMS OF STRESS

Stress affects our minds as well, and, again, typically not in helpful ways. Tasha was forgetful in part because of the negative impact of stress on her brain. Although there is a point at which stress can increase alertness and concentration, when we feel overwhelmed our minds are clouded with anxiety and swirling thoughts that get in the way of us being able to focus. It also means we are preoccupied with analyzing scenarios which may never occur, taking up valuable mental resources, and preventing us from being able to give attention to problem-solving related to the here and now. The symptoms below may reflect the ways in which stress impacts you. Check off those symptoms which apply when you are stressed out.

__Trouble thinking clearly

__Forgetfulness

__Lack of creativity

__Loss or lessening of your sense of humor

__Difficulty making decisions

__Constant worrying

__Cloudy thinking

__Getting distracted easily

__Difficulty finding the words to express yourself

__Difficulty staying tuned into conversations

__Making more mistakes in your arithmetic or writing

---

**Key Concept:** *"Four areas of life affected by stress are Mental, Physical, Emotional, and Behavioural."*

---

# DAY 5 WORKSHEET

## *REACT*

1. Were you aware of these different ways that we can respond to stress?

What would you have predicted prior to this section in terms of the way that you respond to stress?

## *REFLECT*

1. Look at the symptoms in the PHYSICAL category again. Rate each of them (from 0-5) in terms of how often they have bothered you the past week.

       0=Never

       1=Rarely

       2=Sometimes

       3=Slightly LESS than 50% of the time

       4=Slightly MORE than 50% of the time

       5=Almost all the time

__Headaches

__Indigestion

__Stomach aches

__Sweaty palms

__Dizziness

__Nausea

__Back, Neck, Shoulder, or other muscle tightness or pain

__Jaw pain, possibly from clenching your teeth

__Racing heart

__Restlessness

__Tiredness

__Sleep problems (can't get to sleep, interrupted sleep, or early awakening)

__Nightmares

_____ TOTAL (MAX 65) - PHYSICAL SYMPTOMS

2. Look at the symptoms in the EMOTIONAL category again. Rate each of them (from 0-5) in terms of how often they have bothered you the past week. (Rating scale same as first section.)

\_\_Nervousness or anxiety

\_\_Tearfulness, or feeling like you are on the brink of crying

\_\_Edginess or feeling like you are ready to snap at others or explode

\_\_Feeling powerless or helpless

\_\_Feeling under pressure

\_\_Loneliness

\_\_Having a "hair trigger" or getting upset very quickly or easily

\_\_Feeling unhappy and not being able to identify why

\_\_Feeling chronic annoyance

\_\_Feeling chronic boredom

\_\_Feeling like nothing is important or meaningful

\_\_Feeling "flat" and no longer taking pleasure in things

\_\_Feeling distant from everyone, like you're behind a glass wall.

\_\_\_\_\_ TOTAL (MAX 65) - EMOTIONAL SYMPTOMS

3. Look at the symptoms in the BEHAVIOURAL category again. Rate each of them (from 0-5) in terms of how often they have bothered you the past week. (Rating scale same as first section.)

___Drinking more or too much

___Using any other drugs to "self medicate" stress or make you feel "ok"

___Compulsive eating or eating to change your mood

___Grinding your teeth

___Smoking more or compulsively

___Bossing others around

___Arguing with others or picking fights

___Criticizing others

___Not getting daily tasks at home or work completed

___Sleeping too much

_____ TOTAL (MAX 40) - BEHAVIOURAL SYMPTOMS

4. Look at the symptoms in the MENTAL category again. Rate each of them (from 0-5) in terms of how often they have bothered you the past week. (Rating scale same as first section.)

\_\_Trouble thinking clearly

\_\_Forgetfulness

\_\_Lack of creativity

\_\_Loss or lessening of your sense of humor

\_\_Difficulty making decisions

\_\_Constant worrying

\_\_Cloudy thinking

\_\_Getting distracted easily

\_\_Difficulty finding the words to express yourself

\_\_Difficulty staying tuned into conversations

\_\_Making more mistakes in your arithmetic or writing

\_\_\_\_\_ TOTAL (MAX 55) – MENTAL SYMPTOMS

## RESPOND

1. Today, make a note of the symptoms that you have just evaluated. Can you notice in the way that stress has affected you over the years? Re-do the test at the end of the day to see how your symptoms change.

# DAY 6: PERSONAL STRESS PROFILE

## SUMMARY AND STRESS PROFILE

Now that you've had a chance to find out more about stress, and how it affects you, you can start putting together a stress profile for yourself. Basically, this is a simple way of summarizing the types of things that create your stress, and how you typically respond to stress.

Let's go back to Tasha, the lady from the earlier example. Her primary source of stress may be vocational - workplace stress. In this case, it could be managing workload – maybe she forgot to check on the agenda to see what files were most important to focus on and she overlooked the one related to the client coming the next morning. On the other hand, maybe her boss is simply being a jerk, and shuffling responsibilities on to her unfairly. Perhaps Tasha has had conflict with her boss in the past when she has resisted unfair demands, and been threatened to be fired if she didn't get things done. It could also be that Tasha has been feeling badly about not spending as much time with her family since her new promotion, and what is really stressing her out is the strained relationships she now has with her family members. Perhaps it is her overspending that is forcing her to take a managerial position that demands more of her time, in which case, it could be that the financial category is most significant. In any case, if there is a theme that is emerging re: the source of stress, it can inform the steps that Tasha may wish to take to deal with it. It is only when we identify the underlying source of stress that we can start to understand what may need to change in order to reduce that stress.

## ANSWERING THE 3 QUESTIONS

So, by the end of this section you should now know the answers to the questions we were asking at the beginning:

1. What is stress?

2. What is your stress? (The primary source(s) of it?)

3. How does your stress affect you? (What symptoms do you experience most often?)

If you've been able to answer these questions, then you are set to move on to the next section – understanding the underlying dynamics of stress so that we can ultimately learn to reduce or eliminate the feeling of being 'stressed out' altogether.

---

**Key Concept:** *"You should now be able to answer the three questions. What is stress? What is your stress? How does your stress affect you?"*

---

# DAY 6 WORKSHEET

## *REACT*

1. Do you believe that this section has helped you identify your stress? What were you the most surprised by in this section?

## *REFLECT*

1. In terms of your own stress profile, how do you feel about pinpointing the key elements that contribute to your stress levels?

2. Knowing your tendencies now, what are the ways that you can alert yourself to times when your stress level is rising?

   1.

   2.

   3.

3. Who are the people in your world that could provide you some feedback that would let you know when your stress is rising? What would you tell them to look out for?

## *RESPOND*

1. In the next few days, make an effort to predict when your stress levels are likely to rise, based on your stress profile.

2. Invite those people you identified in question 4 to bring to your attention when your stress is increasing.

3. Chart the extent to which being aware of your stress before it gets too high can contribute to managing it better. Be creative!

*CONGRATULATIONS!* You've just finished the first section of the training, and addressed the first issue relating to "Identifying Your Stress." Now it's time to move on the next section.

Part 2:

# UNDERSTANDING STRESS

# DAY 7: WHAT'S BEHIND STRESS: EMOTIONS

## OUTLINE OF UNDERSTANDING STRESS

In the course of this next section we will be answering three important questions that will help us better understand how to deal with stress. We want to really deal with the core issues creating our stress, but to do that we need to go 'behind the scenes' to discover what's going on. If you've seen the ending of the movie the Wizard of Oz, you will remember how this big scary Wizard, was actually a small little man behind a screen. We want to expose stress for what it really is, particularly when it seems threatening to us. Dealing with symptoms isn't enough anymore. We are wanting to discover the heart of the matter.

We begin by asking "What's behind stress?". What we're really looking to find out is whether a common element exists between stress and other negative emotions which are typically linked to it. Once we determine that, we will be in a better position to figure out why there always seems to be a pattern to our stress and that it keeps cycling round and round. Finally, once we identify the stress cycle we will want to figure out what we can use to help get us out of it.

## UNDERLYING SOURCE OF STRESS

Finding out about your own personal stress profile may be helpful, but you want to be able to manage your stress better, right? There's nothing wrong with that. Plenty of people will feel better after taking time to do some deep breathing exercises, go to a yoga class, or have a relaxing bath. These can be effective temporarily. However, it's time to think outside the box. What if there was another way to handle stress? Not necessarily a series of relaxation techniques and exercises designed to help you combat symptoms, but rather a whole new approach to stress management where we actually attack the root cause of our experience of 'being stressed' and eliminate it entirely. If that was possible, it would change everything – wouldn't it?

Imagine having the power to live a life in which you could constantly adapt to changes occurring around and inside of you without ever reaching a point at which you became 'stressed out.' Most people would crave such an opportunity, and yet it doesn't seem possible. Actually, that's wrong! We are going to introduce you to a few key principles that will change your life. There are simple steps that you can take right now that will make this a reality. Your first step is to understand stress – let's start there.

## STRESS IS LIKE AN EMOTION

Stress is often felt and experienced as an emotion, even though it's more than that. However, understanding that stress can function as an emotion is helpful if it can assist us in reducing or eliminating stress. Emotions are tricky things to understand, because we think that they just 'happen' to us. Actually, they are 'created,' and understanding how they are created is important on your journey towards getting rid of your stress. We've broken it down to a three-step process.

**STEP 1:** You have an expectation of what can or should be happening around you, to you, or inside of you.

**STEP 2:** Your life unfolds – often in a way that you might not have wanted or expected.

**STEP 3:** You interpret what just happened on the basis of what you thought could or should be happening.

RESULT = EMOTIONS!

---

**Key Concept:** *"Stress is often felt and experienced as an emotion, even though it is more than that..."*

---

# DAY 7 WORKSHEET

## REACT

1. What is your reaction to this description of emotions? Why do you agree or disagree?

## REFLECT

1. Identify three times when you have had the sequence just outlined happen in your own life.

    1.

    2.

    3.

2. Do you think this sequence happens more often with positive or negative emotions? Why?

# DAY 8: WHAT'S BEHIND STRESS: DESIRES

## BIRTHDAY GIFT SURPRISE

Here's an example. Let's imagine that you are a six year old kid getting ready for your birthday. You have been hinting to your parents that you'd REALLY like a certain toy. The big day arrives, and you see a big box wrapped up with a bow on it that is the EXACT size of the toy you're hoping for. The time comes to open the present and you eagerly tear open the wrapping paper. Your excitement has reached its peak. You open the package and see your beloved toy. You are so happy you jump up and down and hug your parents in gratitude. Life is great! You feel wonderful.

Now let's replay that scenario. As you open the package, you see that the box doesn't have the markings of a package from a store. Your previous excitement turns to disappointment when you open it up and realize that instead of the toy that you were looking forward to, it's actually a sweater that your great-aunt knit for you that you know your friends would mock if you ever wore it in public. You struggle to hold back the tears as you realize that the present that you were longing for isn't in the box and that your Mom will likely make you wear your special 'birthday sweater' to school that day. Your life is awful! You feel miserable.

## LATE FOR SUPPER

Here's another example. This time you're an adult with a job. You arrive at work to discover three new files on your desk. Each file represents approximately 2 hours of work. You see a note from your boss on the top that says 'Need these done today!' You cringe as you realize that yesterday's project still has a half day's work left on it, and you promised that you would be home early for your spouse's birthday supper. Half a day = 4 hours. 3 files x 2 hrs per file = 6 hours. Instantly you realize you will be working overtime to try and get everything done. Welcome to stress!

You set to work feverishly trying to get everything done, starting with yesterday's project. Your stress level is rising and you can't concentrate. Your mind is racing as you go over the conversation you're going to have with your partner and the inevitable argument that you will likely have as they get angry at how your work always takes priority over family. Within half an hour, you are a stressed out mess and you haven't been able to make progress on the project. You get up to grab a coffee and run into your boss in the lunch room.

Your boss smiles and asks how the files are coming. You debate lying about how you're on top of it, but instead decide to be honest: "I'm trying to finish off the project from yesterday first, actually," you state. Your boss responds with a quizzical look, and says "Didn't you see the email I sent last night? The files are top priority because the client is coming in at five to pick them up. You can finish the project tomorrow." Instantly your stress disappears as you realize you'll still have time to get them done and still see your spouse for supper.

## WHAT WE WANT

What actually just happened? Let's go behind the story to analyze things a bit. First let's understand that we all as humans have things that we want to have happen. These things that we want may be legitimate needs – things like food, water, and shelter. There's nothing wrong with wanting those. We may even want other things that are good that aren't as essential. These include things we just discussed like the birthday present, or to get home from work on time for a special dinner. Nothing wrong with those either.

But here is the tricky part about the things that we want – if we had the ability to get everything we wanted, whenever we wanted, we probably would have done so by now. I want a new car – voila, I go and buy it with the stash of cash I have sitting in my sock drawer. I want a promotion, so I tell the owner of the company to change my position and they do so without hesitation. I want my spouse to treat me better or to spend more time with me creating romance, and it happens instantly. I tell my kids to obey me without fail and they start listening to me immediately. Unfortunately, life just doesn't work like that! That's not reality!

If we could always get what we want, our lives would be much different than they are now and we would feel differently, too. Somehow our wants are connected to our emotions and can influence how we feel. This is why we need to understand what's going on under the surface that creates the different emotions that we have every day. Once we understand this process we can use it to rid our lives of stress – and that's what you are here to learn!

## DESIRES EXPLAINED

So we need to take the idea of wants and use it to help define what we are going to call DESIRES. Now, there are many definitions for desires, but ultimately they all take into account a deep longing that we have for things to happen in our lives. We are going to define desires as: "Things that we want to have happen that we don't fully control." Based on that definition, we all have lots of desires in many different areas of our lives.

Physically, I might want to be in great shape so I can be a professional basketball player. However, I don't fully control whether or not any NBA teams are willing to sign to a contract a 47 year old guy who hasn't even played basketball in college. Emotionally, I might want to be happy 24/7, but things frequently go wrong in my life which prevent that from happening. Mentally, I want to be able to focus and concentrate without stopping for eight hours in a row but my mind doesn't seem to cooperate with me the way I want it to. I have desires for many areas of my life, and I bet you do too.

---

**Key Concept:** *"Desires are things in our lives that we want to happen, but we don't fully control."*

---

Having desires is not the problem. They seem to be there

whether we want them to be or not. Many of us wouldn't be able to imagine a day where we would wake up in the morning without any desires. If we had no desires at all, we would probably just stay in bed and stare at the ceiling. There would be nothing to motivate us, nothing to give us meaning and purpose, and nothing to move us forward. I think we would all agree that this is not our picture of a fulfilling life. We aren't designed as humans to function that way!

## 1. SEVEN DESIRE CATEGORIES

Because we have made a link between our desires and how we feel, it's important to become aware of them and identify some of the desires you may have in each of the major areas of your life. By breaking down your life into specific areas, it becomes easier to identify these desires. There are seven major areas to think about:

1. Physical

2. Emotional

3. Mental

4. Spiritual

5. Relational

6. Vocational

7. Financial

Once you take the time to go through each of these areas it will open your eyes to all of the wants and desires you have that you may not even be aware of. Again, this awareness is your first step to freedom from stress! So...stick with us here.

# DAY 8 WORKSHEET

## *REACT*

1. What do you think of the author's definition of desires?

## *REFLECT*

1. If you agree with how desires are being described, list some of your own desires. Here are some categories to get you started:

**Physical**

1. Health

2. Strength

3. Attractiveness

4. Other

**Emotional**

1. Freedom from negative emotions – which emotions?

2. Freedom to feel happy

3. Emotionally stable and secure

4. Other

**Mental**

1. Memory

2. Concentration

3. Intelligence

4. Other

**Spiritual**

1. Meaning

2. Purpose

3. Morality

4. Other

**Relational**

1. Give love – to whom?

2. Receive love – from whom?

3. Stronger, stable relationship – with whom?

4. Other

**Vocational**

1. Utility - doing something useful

2. Competency - being good at it

3. Stability - being in a job that is secure

4. Other

**Financial**

1. Debt-free

2. Living well

3. Security

4. Other

**RESPOND**

1. Look for desires in other areas of your life. Jot them down in your journal.

# DAY 9: WHAT'S BEHIND STRESS: REACTIONS
## DOUBLE-EDGED SWORD

You've had a chance to think about all of the things that you want in your life. That's probably quite a wish list! Even Santa might have a tough time coming through with all of those items, even if you have been nice this year! Now, I don't want to change this list for you, because it's probably a good one that reflects the things that are important to you, and which motivate you. And when you get what you want, you feel great! When you ace that test at school, get that promotion at work, or the person you're interested in wants to go on a date with you – in all these situations you will probably feel wonderful! If you were always feeling wonderful, you probably wouldn't be reading this book right now, though.

So desires are normal, and healthy and we feel good when they are met. But desires are a bit of a double-edge sword. We need to understand what typically happens to us if we don't get the things that we really want, or at least as fast as we would like to get them. In other words, what is our emotional response when our desires aren't met? Understanding this is the next step in dealing with stress.

## REACTIONS TO UNMET DESIRES

In working with clients for over 20 years, we've observed that these emotional responses to unmet desires tend to go down three primary pathways, which we call the three "A's." Let's talk about what those are right now.

## ANXIOUS

Sometimes there is uncertainty surrounding your desires. You say to yourself: "I hope this happens. I want it to happen. It needs to happen." But the uncertainty around whether the desire will be met typically makes you feel scared, worried, concerned or pressured. Let's say I have to take an exam tomorrow and I'm not going to have much time to study for it. All day, I am feeling stressed as a result. While I'm studying, I'm feeling apprehensive. When I'm taking the test, I'm feeling angst. When I'm waiting to get the marks back to see how well I did, I'm feeling anxious. No one likes these feelings.

## ANGRY

Now if someone or something is blocking you from having your desire met, you can get mad or upset. You start feeling frustrated, angry and eventually bitter and resentful. You are now angry at this situation or the person that's getting in the way of you getting what you want. Imagine trying to concentrate on a project at work. Your co-worker is humming to himself at the cubicle next to you. You ask him nicely to stop. He turns and stares at you without saying a word. Then he turns back and continues to hum again. You are likely starting to feel angry at him.

## AWFUL

When something you've been looking forward to having happen doesn't, and it looks as though it might never happen, you can start feeling disappointed and discouraged. You may also begin to feel helpless and hopeless, like it doesn't matter what you do or how much you try, you'll never have your desire met. Now you may eventually feel despair and depression. You feel awful and sad. Imagine someone who secretly has had feelings for a friend, but has been too shy to express that they want to establish a romantic relationship with them. One day they find out that their friend is engaged. They instantly realize that their feelings for their friend will likely never be returned. Depressing, isn't it!

---

**Key Concept:** *"Desires are a bit of a double-edged sword. We need to understand what typically happens to us when we don't get the things we want..."*

---

## OUR RESPONSE

Now, it is clear that we all experience some of these emotions, and every one of these can be experienced as a form of stress, as they are our response to demands that we or others are placing on us. Since this is a course on stress, presumably you experience more of these emotions than you'd like. Nobody wants more of the negative emotions I've just listed. No one wakes up on Monday morning and says: "This week, my focus is on increasing my anxiety level!" Or "This week I want more frustration in my life!" The very thought of that is silly. Here are a few things that we can all agree on:

1. Negative emotions suck!

2. More of them is bad, fewer of them is better!

3. None of them would be perfect!

# DAY 9 WORKSHEET

## *REACT*

1. What is your response to the three pathways? Which of these do you typically travel down the most?


## REFLECT

1. Describe how unmet desires create ANXIETY for you in the following areas:

1. Home


2. Work


3. Relationships

2. Describe how unmet desires FRUSTRATE or ANGER you in the following areas:

1. Home




2. Work




3. Relationships




3. Describe how unmet desires DEPRESS or DISAPPOINT you in the following areas:

1. Home




2. Work




3. Relationships

# DAY 10: WHAT IS THE STRESS SPIRAL?: STUCK

## WHAT IS THE STRESS SPIRAL?

Now that we understand a little better what may be behind negative emotions, including stress, we can move forward to the next question. We will find out more about the stress spiral and how it works, and our typical responses to it.

First of all, here's the problem – and it's likely the reason that you are probably reading this right now. The problem is that we get stuck trying to get rid of the negative emotions we don't like and we don't know how to get unstuck. I mean, everyone in the world would love to be able to just snap their fingers when they're feeling 'crappy', and instantly feel happy instead. That would be great! But as far as I know, nobody has that superpower! So we obviously don't control our emotions the way we want to, at least not 100% of the time.

So I believe that there are three fundamental truths that we need to understand and accept before we can move forward to how to 'de-stress yourself' which is what you really want to know.

> **Truth 1:** All humans have desires
>
> **Truth 2:** Unmet desires produce stressful feelings
>
> **Truth 3:** We don't have full control of our feelings

## UNDERSTANDING THE PROBLEM

So what are the implications of those truths we just outlined. The most important thing to understand is that when we try to change our negative emotions – things we don't fully control – we are actually generating DESIRES. Remember the definition from before? Desires are things that we want, but we don't fully control. Now, because we don't fully control our emotions, when we try to change them we generate desires. These desires could be unmet because we don't have the tools, resources or understanding to change our emotions the way that we want, and, voila! We have unmet desires which produce, you guessed it, more negative emotions! This, in turn, increases our desire to get rid of these additional negative emotions, and round and round we go. We are well and truly stuck feeling negative emotions, and feeling more anxious, angry or awful the longer that negative cycle continues.

---

**Key Concept:** *"Alll humans have desires. Desires create stressful feelings. We don't have full control over our desires."*

---

## BATHTUB DRAIN

Think of it this way. If you've ever had a bath before, you know that there is typically a drain which, in older tubs, will have a plug in it to stop the water from flowing out. If the plug is bumped aside or removed, the water starts draining immediately, and typically forms a spiral like a mini-tornado as it disappears down the hole. That spiral is a lot like what happens with us and our negative emotions sometimes. We try to stop our emotions, but things keep getting worse and we are feeling drained at the same time. What to do?

# DAY 10 WORKSHEET

## *REACT*

1. What is your response to this description of the negative spiral? Do you think this spiral is an accurate way to describe what happens to you sometimes? Why or why not?

REFLECT

1. Describe the last time you felt stuck in this negative cycle.

2. How frequently does this occur, and when?

3. What is the most common situation in which you feel stuck?

RESPOND

1. The next time that you are starting to spiral down emotionally, stop and describe how you are feeling in your journal.

# DAY 11: WHAT IS THE STRESS SPIRAL?: EXTINGUISH

## HOW WE DEAL WITH STRESS

We humans have a few ways in order to deal with getting unstuck – to stop the bathtub from draining (so to speak) and to de-stress ourselves. I call them the 3 "E's" for lack of a better term. They all start with the letter E which makes them easy to remember.

## EXTINGUISH

The first option for many people when they feel stressed is to try and extinguish or 'suppress' their negative emotions. The idea behind this is that if we can pretend that we aren't feeling the way that we are, then the negative emotions will not bother us anymore. If we don't let our emotions come to the surface, then they won't actually exist!

We can just try to 'put on a happy face' and everything will be better, right? Actually, this doesn't work, and it's exhausting! Unfortunately, our emotions are real and they exist whether or not we want them to, and they will interfere with our life even if we try to extinguish them. Think of this like someone trying to blow out a 'trick' candle on a birthday party cake. They think the flame has disappeared, but it keeps coming back!

## EXTINGUISH EXAMPLE

This reminds me of the time that I (Vern) almost burned down our house... and it really was as bad as it sounds. Our family had returned from a long trip, and I was supposed to be starting supper and getting the kids ready for bed while Calista was out getting some groceries. Instead of heating up a pot of water in order to cook pasta, I ended accidentally turning on an element on the stove that had a plastic kettle sitting on it. My son, who was 6 at the time, asked me what the noise was downstairs. I entered the kitchen to see clouds of black smoke billowing from the stove and heard the smoke alarm going off. As my kids headed to safety outside I tried to figure out how to stop the fire. I grabbed the fire extinguisher from the counter and unloaded it on the fire. Success — I thought. But after briefly suppressing the flames, they burst forth again burning as hard as before. I rushed up stairs to grab another extinguisher and unloaded it onto the fire as well. Still no success! I called 911 and was put on hold (yes, hold!) as I watched helplessly as the flames started to lick their way up toward the oak cupboards and certain disaster. The fire truck was finally notified of our address and I rushed to the basement to kill the breaker for the stove in hopes that would reduce the heat and the flames. I grabbed the last fire extinguisher on my way up and finally doused the fire for good, minutes before the fire fighters arrived. What's my point? Trying to extinguish the fire was difficult until I addressed the underlying issue of the heat from the element causing the flames.

    This is what happens to our emotions if we try to pretend they don't exist. By trying to stuff our feelings down, we may feel like we are doing those around us a favor, but we're not. The impact on others is two-fold. When we don't acknowledge we're stressed, angry or upset with someone, usually that underlying negative feeling will come out in indirect or passive-aggressive behavior or words. People can usually sense that things aren't okay, even if we say we're 'fine', which can create more tension with them, and even more stress for us. Or, eventually it can build up emotional pressure to the point where we end up exploding at someone without a good reason. This also creates more problems and more stress! If this is one way that you tend to deal with emotions you would rather not have, you know what I'm talking about. There must be a healthier way!

---

**Key Concept:** *"When we don't acknowledge we are stressed, angry or upset with someone, usually the underlying feeling will come out in an indirect or passive-aggressive behaviour."*

---

# DAY 11 WORKSHEET

## REACT

1. Do you agree that 'stuffing' our emotions is a typical reaction for people? Why or why not?

2. Do you think that the author's description and opinion of this way of dealing with emotions is accurate?

## REFLECT

1. Describe the times when you have tried to extinguish your negative emotions.

2. What effect does that have on your resource levels? How often do you get exhausted from trying to pretend that everything's okay?

3. Did that work in the end? Do you or others notice that your emotions tend to still 'leak-out' even if you're trying to suppress them?

4. What are the things that tend to cause you to burst your emotional bubble?




5. What are the aftereffects if you happen to explode?




## RESPOND

1. The next time that you find yourself trying to extinguish your negative emotions, make a note of it and try to identify the pattern.

# DAY 12: WHAT IS THE STRESS SPIRAL?: EXPRESS

## EXPRESS

There are many who feel like if they are feeling upset they just need to "let it out" and express the way that they feel instead of keeping it inside.

While there is something to be said for a catharsis, or "release" of emotions, if the emotions are being generated by stress, and the stress isn't being dealt with, just "releasing" is NOT going to solve anything. You may feel better momentarily, but, again, there are consequences.

If all you are doing is "expressing" you will eventually run into one of two problems. 1. We may say things when we're upset that could be hurtful and we regret what we've said. 2. People don't typically want to continually listen to others expressing negative emotions!

The more you try and talk about your anxiety or anger or depression, the less likely it is that those individuals in your support network will want to be there for you. Initially it could be that they just don't know what to say to help you, but after a while you may feel like your support network is avoiding you (which actually may be happening!).

It will not help you to think that people are rejecting you – particularly if you're stressed and want support. Soon feelings of hurt, frustration and anger may be added to your original emotions and the negative cycle will spiral down again.

## EXPRESS EXAMPLE

Here's an example for you. Harry works in an office as a bookkeeper for a medium size operation. The office manager, Frank, who hired him, seemed like a nice enough guy – six months ago! – and Harry had been enjoying his new position. One month ago, however, things began to change. A shift in the economy and a new, very successful advertising campaign launch by their biggest competitor, had really started to take its toll on Harry's company's finances – and on Frank. As things began to worsen, so did Frank's mood. He became loud and negative – ripping into his employees publically and slamming office doors. Harry became Frank's 'sounding board' and on a daily basis Harry heard all the dirt about the company and its employees. Frank was angry and upset and didn't know how to handle the pressure he was feeling to turn the business around. And Harry? Well Harry just wanted to quit to get away from Frank. Poor Frank. It's not his fault how he was feeling. And it's good to talk out feelings. But unless he is talking in a safe place with the purpose of finding a solution, he is just making things worse by driving any support away.

---

**Key Concept:** *Hurt, frustration and anger may be added to your already negative emotions should your support group distance themselves from you."*

# DAY 12 WORKSHEET

## *REACT*

1. What do you think about the idea that expressing may not always be helpful?

2. What have been the messages you have received growing up about letting your emotions out?

## *REFLECT*

1. Describe a time when you have either let out your emotions or had others express them to you.

2. What were the benefits of you letting them out? How long did those last?

3. In what ways did this end up creating problems between you and the other person?

4. Do you feel that expressing your emotions ever resolves the underlying issue creating them?

5. How does your culture and/or upbringing affect your ability or willingness to express your emotions?

6. How do you determine when expressing your emotions has become too much for another person?

## *RESPOND*

1. There is a benefit to being aware of how we're feeling and expressing that to others, as long as that is a part of a constructive conversation in which the other person is expressing how they feel as well and the discussion is focused on a positive way to address these emotions. Think back to the past month, and identify the number of times when you were expressing your emotions fit into that description.

2. If you feel like you need to vent to someone, ask the person to let you know when they have reached their limit. This will be simple step you can take to minimize the negative effects of expressing your emotions.

# DAY 13: WHAT IS THE STRESS SPIRAL?: ESCAPE

## ESCAPE

Attempting to escape a negative spiral is understandable. If you feel stressed, you want relief. I think there are three primary ways to escape from negative emotions, including stress. We're going to talk about them now. They include:

1. Physical Escape

2. Emotional Escape

3. Psychological Escape

## PHYSICAL ESCAPE

If someone or something is causing me to feel negative emotions by blocking me from achieving my desire, then I probably want to get away! I can sometimes physically distance myself from a person by avoiding them. Usually, however, the person or situation I'm trying to get away from is in my life for a reason, and therefore an escape is difficult. Also, avoiding can often cause more problems!

It's hard to avoid your boss and your job, or your spouse and your kids if those are part of the problem for you. Ultimately, physically leaving or avoiding them is a temporary escape. There are other escape options that are more positive. Sometimes we can only get away for a little while, but it seems to make a difference.

Millions of people use prayer and meditation to quiet their minds and distract themselves from emotional turmoil. They report feeling better after spending time in a quiet place relaxing. Others choose a more physical route and use yoga or exercise to relieve their stress. They report feeling more energy or getting a boost of the 'runner's high' and endorphin release that comes from exercise.

There's nothing wrong with any of these options. However, none of these address the root of why we're feeling the way we are. Until we get at the source, we will simply be 'managing stress,' not eliminating stress altogether.

## EMOTIONAL ESCAPE

Sometimes people feel overwhelmed with emotions they can't handle. When that happens they can emotionally shut down, or stop caring. Others put up emotional walls that prevent others from knowing what's going on inside of them. Some clients describe going numb and disconnecting entirely from their emotional selves, just going through the motions, and functioning without feeling.

The reality is that it is difficult to escape emotionally because it typically leads to isolation and a loss of connection in relationships. Feeling like you can't be close to others that you actually love and care about can create its own problems, such as the loneliness.

Ultimately, this loneliness can prompt a drive to reconnect. But reconnection without having addressed the underlying issue that initially prompted the escape, still doesn't solve the problem any more than a physical escape would. The cycle will continue unless other changes are made.

## PSYCHOLOGICAL ESCAPE PART 1

The final way that people escape is to go to a different place in their mind. In our culture we tend to want relief sooner rather than later. Well if you are in the market for instant relief, you have plenty of options. This is the pathway of addiction. There are many options in terms of escape routes here – we've divided them into nine S's:

**1. SUBSTANCES:** Drugs and alcohol are a quick fix.

**2. SCREENS:** Finding a pleasant distraction through technology and using screens to watch TV, play video games, or go on social media sites is increasingly common these days.

**3. SHOPPING:** Some find a pleasant escape in the thrill of seeking out a purchase at the mall

**4. SUGAR / SALT:** Frequently when we eat sugary or fatty foods to escape emotional pain we experience a psychological escape.

**5. SEX:** Some people become addicted to the intense feelings associated with sex or being 'in love' and will lose themselves in short-term sexual relationships or find temporary escape in pornography.

**6. SPECULATING:** Gambling or betting is another way to find temporary excitement.

**7. SOCIALIZING:** Sometimes we like to go out to 'party' as a means to escape the way we feel.

**8. SWEATING:** We go workout to get an endorphin rush –

healthy yes, but still temporary.

**9. SLEEP:** We may go to bed instead of facing an unpleasant reality when we're awake.

What do all of these have in common? With the exception of sleep, they all work the same way. They stimulate pleasure centers in the brain. In doing so, they provide temporary relief quickly from negative emotions.

## PSYCHOLOGICAL ESCAPE PART 2

On the down side, this temporary relief comes at a cost and doesn't solve the problem. Those of you who are familiar with the destructive impact of addiction can identify with the fact that people are typically motivated to go and 'use' drugs or alcohol when they are feeling low, as a means of trying to escape feeling awful. That's one of the problems with substance use – it is extremely effective at accomplishing this task – but it's a temporary fix.

When someone comes down from their high or sobers up, they don't typically feel better than they did before – they feel worse! Relationships and jobs suffer, leaving people lonelier and more frustrated.

Shame or guilt could be added to the host of negative emotions those who are escaping are feeling already, and voila! The cycle of negative emotions continues until the next time when they can't handle how they're feeling, and go escape again.

In all cases, when we escape we aren't solving the problem.

Just like escaping from a house fire is good, in that it allows us relief from the flames, the ultimate solution is to address the source of the fire and put it out!!

## ULTIMATE GOAL – ELIMINATE STRESS

The ultimate goal is to eliminate the stress that we are stuck in! When that happens, we can live our live in freedom and be the best that we are created to be. That's the hopeful part. That's the exciting part! That's why you are going through this book!! So... let's go!

---

**Key Concept:** *"There are three types of ways individuals escape from negative emotions. They are physical, emotional and psychological. Remember, escaping the burning house is important, but the root of the problem is to stop the house from continuing to burn."*

---

# DAY 13 WORKSHEET

***Note: Yes , it's a long worksheet. But don't stress out! Only do it after you finished the book if it's too much right now. It's not going anywhere!

## *REACT*

1. Do you agree that we all try to escape our negative emotions in some way?

2. Do you think it's healthy to escape sometimes?

## *REFLECT*

### PHYSICAL ESCAPE

1. Describe times when you have avoided a situation or a person:

**At work**

1. Boss

2. Co-worker

3. Overwhelmed with a full 'in-box'

**At home**

1. Person

2. Spouse/Partner

3. Sibling/Parent/Child

**Other relationships**

1. Situation

2. Responsibility

3. Confrontation

2. What was the result of the avoidance?

3. Did you have to eventually deal with that person or situation? Did your avoidance make things better or worse?

**EMOTIONAL ESCAPE**

1. Describe a time when you have emotionally shut down.

2. What does that look like for you?

3. When are you most likely to shut down?

4. Aside from temporary escape, does that eventually make you feel disconnected from others and lonely?

## PSYCHOLOGICAL ESCAPE

1. Describe the times when you have used the following ways to escape:

**1. Substances** – drugs/alcohol/smoking

**2. Screens** – spending time distracting yourself on a computer, phone or TV

**3. Sex** – pornography/masturbation/casual sexual encounters

**4. Shopping** – buying things that you don't need for the 'thrill'

**5. Sugar / Salt** – usually high sugar or fatty foods provide stimulation in the pleasure center of our brains

**6. Speculating** – involving yourself in situations like gambling or betting on races or sports where there is a high risk/reward ratio

**7. Socializing** – going out to 'party' to escape the way you feel

**8. Sweating** – going to workout to get an endorphin rush – healthy, but temporary

**9. Sleep** – going to bed instead of facing reality when you're awake

2. When are you most likely to seek an escape to a different place in your mind?

3. Describe a time when you felt like you were escaping in ways that were negatively affecting your life or relationships.

## *RESPOND*

1. Assess your willingness to look at other ways to deal with the underlying issue creating a need for escape. Assess your willingness to change on a scale from 1-10 where 10 is a strong commitment to change starting today. If you are lower than 5 out of 10, write down the obstacles that are preventing you from moving forward.

2. Commit to journaling at the end of the day the times and ways that you have escaped.

3. Make a chart to document your patterns over a typical week. Becoming aware of when, why and how you escape is an important step in making changes

4. Discuss with a trusted friend or family member the ways that you escape, and invite them to let you know when they notice you starting to escape so that you can increase your level of accountability.

# DAY 14: WHAT CAN WE USE TO GET OUT OF IT?" PART 1

## WHAT CAN WE USE TO GET OUT OF THE STRESS SPIRAL?

So far we've taken a look at emotions, and discovered that negative emotions, including stress, come from unmet desires. Trying to change our emotions isn't as easy as we want it to be, and we can sometimes get stuck in a negative spiral that we try to get out of in a number of ways that ultimately aren't effective. Now we will look at some powerful ways to step out of the 'stress spiral' – for good!!!!!!

## CHRISTMAS SURPRISE

We'll start by imagining a scenario. Let's say you go out Christmas shopping, excited to find a gift for your friend. The mall is beautifully decorated and you are enjoying the holiday tunes, and the festive feelings.

It's a busy day in the mall, and as you're approaching your store you're surprised to see a young man coming toward you with an intense look on his face, with his arms outstretched. Before you can get out of the way, he has pushed you over, and you fall backwards to the ground. Stunned, and with little time to brace yourself, you feel your hips smash onto the floor, and a shot of pain follows. WHAT THE HECK!!!??? Your mind is spinning.

Let's take a moment to check in. How are you feeling? Are you still enjoying the happy feelings you started with? Chances are they might have changed to feelings of shock, confusion, or even anger. Your excitement has left the building, and been replaced almost instantaneously with a negative emotion. It's not hard to see why - you have every right to feel angry!

Now, here's a twist for you. From your place on the floor you look up to see your attacker continue to stumble past you with his arms outstretched. You watch in horror as he crumbles into a pile on the floor, and then starts going into an epileptic seizure. People rush to his side before you can get yourself up and head his way also.

How are you feeling now? Chances are that you are feeling different again than you were a few moments earlier. You're still in pain, but I bet anger has given way to some degree of compassion or concern as you realize what's going on and seek to request medical assistance by calling 911 or mall security.

As you reflect back quickly, it may shock you to realize that your emotions have changed over the past few seconds from joyful anticipation to anger to concern. The question is: What is the mechanism of action that has allowed your emotions to change so quickly, in this example? In other words, how is it possible that our emotions have shifted so dramatically in such a short time, when they can get so stuck sometimes?

## QUICK SHIFT #1 – WHY?

Let's back up and walk our way through this example to see if we can find out what important element has changed. Your physical circumstances did change during the first shift – you were unexpectedly pushed down. However, between the shift from anger to concern, nothing changed. You were still on your butt in the middle of the mall, having been pushed down by a complete stranger, and yet you were feeling entirely different about things. Why?

While at first you thought he was attacking you – in which case you would have been justified in feeling anger towards them. When you realized, however, that he was just trying to brace himself because he was about to fall down and have a seizure, and you just happened to be in the way, then you didn't feel angry – you were now concerned.

We need to look at your perception of the attacker's intention. Before you thought he was attacking on purpose. Then you realized it was an accident. Instantly your emotions changed to be consistent with your new perception of the "attacker's" intention. In fact, it would be difficult, if not impossible for you to go back to feeling angry toward the guy. Your perceptual shift determined your new emotional state.

HERE IS THE IMPORTANT POINT! Our perceptions and thoughts play a huge role in how we experience emotions. This fact is, incidentally, backed by 60 years of research. This is a powerful tool that we can use this to help reduce our experience of stress.

**Key Concept:** *"Perceptions and thoughts play a huge role in how we experience emotions."*

# DAY 14 WORKSHEET

## *REACT*

1. What is your initial reaction to this information? Do you agree with the connection outlined? Why or why not?

## *REFLECT*

1. Describe a time when you had your perception of a situation or a person's motivation change. How did your emotion shift?

2. Describe a time when you have been aware of the connection between perception and emotion.

3. Describe a time when you intentionally tried to alter your perception in order to influence your emotion.

## RESPOND

1. Outline a way in which you could use the information just described to positively impact your life.

2. Describe how you would be able to track those changes.

3. Make a list right now of the things you would like to see happen.

    1.

    2.

    3.

4. How can you begin to take steps towards these changes?

# DAY 15: WHAT CAN WE USE TO GET OUT OF IT? PART 2

## LATE FOR TENNIS

There's another powerful point you need to understand before we can get to work making changes in your life. We will start with another illustration so you can see how it works.

Let's say I've arranged to meet a buddy to play tennis at 7:00 am. I set my alarm for 6:30 but it doesn't go off, and I sleep in. I wake up at 6:55 and I'm not feeling great; I think I might be coming down with something. I'm dreading the prospect of playing, as I just want to go back to sleep. I try to call my buddy's cellphone to postpone our match, but I get his wife instead, because he forgot his phone at home. He'll be stuck waiting for me unless I do something.I decide to jump in the car and drive over to the court to let him know we'll have to reschedule. When I arrive, he asks me to help him by returning some of his serves for a few minutes before I head back home. I agree and start practicing with him.

Within minutes I realize that I am having more success than usual against him (he always wins!) and tell him I want to play. The physical movement is getting my blood pumping and by the end of the match I've come out on top. I feel great – completely different than I did an hour before. The question is why?

## QUICK SHIFT #2 – WHY?

What was it that changed to allow my emotions to shift in this example? It wasn't my perceptions, initially. I was dreading the prospect of going to play tennis. What opened the door for my emotions to shift was something that we all have access to.

First – a choice. Out of loyalty to a commitment that I made to my friend, I made a decision not to leave him hanging. Then, I actually had to act on that – my behavior changed, and all of a sudden I set in motion a series of events that resulted in my positive feelings an hour later.

That is the power of action. Our actions can temporarily override our thoughts, and result in a shift in our emotions. That is another powerful point that we can harness in order to change our negative emotional states into positive ones.

---

**Key Concept:** *"Actions override our thoughts, and result in a shift in our emotions."*

---

# DAY 15 WORKSHEET

## *REACT*

1. What is your initial reaction to this information? Do you agree with the connection outlined? Why or why not?

## *REFLECT*

1. Describe a time when you made a choice and took action in a way that went against the way you were feeling at the time. How did your emotion shift?

2. Describe a time when you have been aware of the connection between actions and emotions before.

3. Describe a time when you intentionally tried to alter your actions in order to influence your emotion.

## RESPOND

1. Outline a way in which you could use the information just described to positively impact your life.

2. Describe how you would be able to track those changes.

3. Make a list right now of the things you would like to see happen.

    1.

    2.

    3.

4. How can you begin to take steps towards these changes?

# DAY 16: UNDERSTANDING STRESS REVIEW (NO WORKSHEET)

## SUMMARY

Let's summarize what we've learned so far (Refer to Appendix 1 at the end of the book for a diagram of preceding content). Our emotions are powerful. By themselves they can influence the way we think, and they can affect our actions. Because we can't snap our fingers and be happy, we try other options: to extinguish, express or escape our emotions. These are temporary fixes and don't address the underlying issues. On the other hand, when we combine the power of our thoughts and our actions, we will be able to overpower our negative emotions, including stress, and make the changes we need to feel better, and live in emotional freedom. So...

## REVIEW

1. We all have desires – things we want to have happen that we don't fully control.

2. Unmet desires produce unwanted emotions, including stress.

3. We don't have full control of our emotions.

THEREFORE:

1. We want to get rid of stress, but that's actually a desire.

2. When we fail to manage our stress we actually feel worse – this can cause a negative spiral.

3. The way out of this is to break into the cycle by using two powerful weapons - our thoughts and our actions.

---

**Key Concept:** *"Desires produce unwanted stress that we cannot control. Wanting to get rid of this stress is a desire, which causes us to feel worse about ourselves. We break through by combining our thoughts and actions."*

---

Part 3:
# REDUCING STRESS

# DAY 17: WHY DO WE NEED A STRESS REGULATOR?: INTRODUCTION

## (NO WORKSHEET)

**REVIEW OF PREVIOUS SECTIONS**

Ok, so we have covered the first two steps towards getting rid of stress. Part 1 focussed on Identifying Stress. We found out what the definition of stress was, the various types of stress, and the different ways that it impacts us: emotionally, physically, behaviorally, and mentally. We discovered that stress can be good or bad, but ultimately it takes its toll on us.

Part 2 focussed on Understanding Stress. We looked at what's behind it, and the definition of desires and the impact that unmet desires can have on our lives. We saw how the stress spiral develops by trying to change our emotions without the necessary resources to do so. We also learned that we can use our perceptions and our actions to break out of that spiral. Ultimately, we know that understanding is important because it's only when we understand stress, and other negative emotions like it, that we can attempt to do something about it. Now it's time for the really good stuff in Section 3: Reducing Stress.

## **OUTLINE OF SECTION 3**

1. Why do we need a stress regulator?

2. What is the stress-cycle?

3. How can we regulate our stress?

## WHY DO WE NEED A STRESS REGULATOR?

We don't want all the stress that we have. If you were managing all of your stress perfectly right now, you probably wouldn't be reading this book! We want it to go away – as in, we don't want to have any stress, because stress is bad, right?

When we sit down and think about it, though, what actually causes us stress? Usually things that are in our life for a reason, like work, family and relationships. Do we really want all of these stress-causing parts of our life to go away? Probably not. We can't even imagine a life without these present, or at least, we wouldn't want to.

---

**Key Concept:** *"Ultimately, we know that understanding is important because it's only when we understand stress, and other negative emotions like it, that we can attempt to do something about it."*

---

Aren't we actually looking for a better way to deal with them? To be able to keep them around, but build our resiliency to stress?

# DAY 18: WHY DO WE NEED A STRESS REGULATOR?: STRESS & PERFORMANCE

## STRESS AND PERFORMANCE

In order to understand exactly what we are looking for, let's look at research by Yerkes & Dodson (1908) which has revealed an interesting feature of the relationship between stress and performance.

**Low stress** = low performance, boredom

**Medium stress** = optimum performance

1. Energized

2. Focussed

3. 'Flow' = effortless work

**High stress** = low performance

1. Fatigue, exhaustion, burnout

Let's take a look at a graph to help us see clearly how this works...

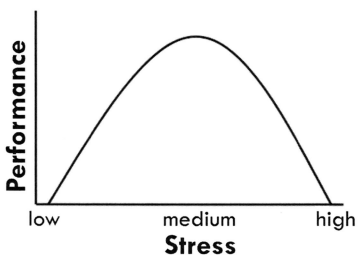

## STRESS AND PERFORMANCE GRAPH

If you look at this graph, you can see illustrated what we just reviewed. We want to be at the high point for performance, but that means that we have to have a certain amount of stress in our lives.

## STRESS AND PERFORMANCE SUMMARY

Okay, so here's what we know - too much stress is bad, and the negative effects of stress are well documented and were reviewed in the first section.

However, as we've discovered, not enough stress leads to a lack of productivity. If there was no deadline for that project at work, would we really get it done in a reasonable timeframe? If there was no bell at the school signaling the first class starting, would we really get our kids there at that time of the morning? If there was no hunger inside of us, would we really stop what we enjoy doing to make a meal for ourselves or our family?

---

**Key Concept:** *"Low stress = boredom, medium stress = optimal performance, high stress = fatigue."*

---

The alternative is to regulate ourselves to achieve. This has been defined as "the ability of a person to voluntarily shift one's state of mind in order to most effectively meet any challenge before them." We need a stress regulator to allow us to function at peak performance without becoming overwhelmed and unproductive. We need to regulate stress in a healthy way to maximize its benefits and minimize its negative effects. In order to do that, however, we need to go behind the scenes again. This time we start with the idea of capacity.

# DAY 18 WORKSHEET

## *REACT*

1. What is your initial reaction to the idea that some stress is necessary?

## *REFLECT*

1. Think of a time in your life (aside from a vacation) where there wasn't much to do (if you have children, perhaps you'll have to think back to a time prior to that!). Describe how your boredom affected your productivity.

Event:

Affect on event:

2. Without some pressure or deadline, what do you think would happen to your performance at work?




3. Describe a time when you were in the 'flow' of the moment when you were focused and effective, but not overwhelmed. In what ways can you relate to the ideas presented?




4. Describe a time when that productivity became compromised by too much stress.

## RESPOND

1. Make a note this week of the times when you are in the 'flow' of peak performance. If it doesn't ever happen to you, take some time to analyze the stress levels you are under to identify possible areas to focus on that will assist you to learn how to reduce your stress.

# DAY 19: WHY DO WE NEED A STRESS REGULATOR?: CAPACITY

## CAPACITY

We are going to start with understanding what we mean by the word 'capacity.' This simple concept will change your life – just wait! The simplest way to understand capacity is to think of a container. How much water can I fit in that container? A cup? A quart? A gallon? 55 gallons? The size of the container determines its capacity – the maximum amount of water it can hold without the water spilling over. I will use an example here to show you how and why this concept is important.

## RAIN BARREL

Imagine you get a 55 gallon rain barrel installed outside to collect the water coming down through the drains from your roof. It has the potential to provide a lot of water that you could use for your garden. That's a lot of water you can use for the garden. That's exciting because you love to garden and you are counting on that water to make your garden beautiful.

But what happens if, a few weeks into the summer, and it hasn't rained recently? You've been happily watering your plants unaware of what's going on inside your barrel. Then one day, there's only a little water there – not nearly enough for you to water your beautiful garden. How disappointing! Here's the thing...

## CHANGING CAPACITY

You might own an awesome huge rain barrel with the Maximum Capacity to hold plenty of water, but that doesn't mean it does today. What the container is actually holding depends on several factors:

1. Whether there's been rain.

2. Whether you've used tons of water for your tomatoes.

3. Whether there's a leak.

What the container is actually holding we will call its Current Capacity. Does that make sense?

## CAPACITY IN AREAS OF LIFE

You might be thinking, "Yes, but what's your point?"

Here's the thing. Every area of our lives can be thought of like a rain barrel. Stick with me here – I know that sounds dumb!)

Now let's see how that can be applied to the four major areas of our lives that we tend to struggle with. These areas of our lives that are impacted by stress, are the physical, emotional, behavioral, and mental. Imagine each of these areas being a barrel – each of them has its own capacity that reflects its maximum size.

Take me for instance. I am tall (6'5") and when I was younger and in shape (25 years ago!), I played volleyball at university. The size of my physical 'barrel' hasn't changed (aside from widening a little!), but my capacity was far fuller then than it is now! If I was to rate my strength, agility, cardio levels and playing ability now, I would have to say that I am probably about 60% of what I was back then. I really haven't worked out daily or done a weight training program since I finished university. If I call my physical ability as a university athlete my 'peak' or maximum capacity, it makes sense that I'm not able to function there now.

So if you asked me if I was at the peak of my capacity now, I'd have to say no. And, to be honest, if I asked you "Do you know of anyone that functions at the peak of their physical capacity, all the time, 24/7?" you answer would probably be, "No!"

---

**Key Concept:** *"Regardless of how big your container is, what you hold right now is a measure of your current functioning. This is called your Current Capacity."*

---

The same could be said for the other areas of our lives, as well. Mentally, emotionally, and spiritually we may have a greater chance of increasing or maintaining our capacity than we do physically. However, there can be times or situations in our lives that cause us to really struggle in those other areas, too. And here's something else to think about! Whether we are talking about physical, emotional, or mental capacity, our level of functioning can change significantly within the same day!

In fact, I don't even think it's possible to be at 100% functioning all the time as humans, regardless of the area of our life. Physically we get sick, tired, or injured. We may have restrictions on us in terms of time and energy levels. And as we age, our physical ability tends to decline. Sadly, I am more aware of now that I am in the middle years!

So, whether physical, emotional, mental or spiritual, our functioning tends to change frequently throughout the day. Maybe in the morning, I feel better physically, but then I tire out as the day goes on. Maybe emotionally I feel terrible in the morning as I face another day at work, and then a co-worker does an unexpected favor for me, and I feel better. Maybe I am able to concentrate in the morning with a fresh cup of coffee inside of me to start the day, but after lunch I find it harder to focus. Stress can affect each of these areas as well, as we've already discovered. What we need to do is look at how stress develops. Once you understand that, you can reduce or eliminate it. Stick with us – we're almost there!

# DAY 19 WORKSHEET

## *REACT*

1. What is your initial reaction to this idea of the natural fluctuation in these four primary areas of functioning? Do you agree that this is true?

2. Do you think it is possible for someone to ever function at maximum levels, even for a short period of time?

## *REFLECT*

1. Let's examine in more depth three areas of functioning in your own life right now. Give and example of a high and a low in the past six months.

**Physical**

1. Ability – the amount of physical abilities you have now compared to when you were at your peak. For instance, you may have been able to run a marathon, but now you may only be able to get to the mailbox!

    1. High

    2. Low

2. Energy – the amount of 'vigor' or 'get up and go' you have. This is also related to your endurance – the ability to sustain that energy over time

    1. High

    2. Low

3. Activity – the amount of time and opportunity you have in your life to be able to spend engaged in physical activities. This could be impacted by a variety of factors.

    1. High

2. Low

**Emotional**

1. Accessibility – reflects your ability to be 'in-touch' with your emotional state, where you can readily identify and respond honestly to how you are feeling at any given moment.

    1. High

    2. Low

2. Stability – refers to your ability to govern your emotional states in ways that prevent them from interfering with situations or relationships in your life.

    1. High

    2. Low

3. Utility – refers to your ability to use your emotions to inform the situation you find yourself in and respond appropriately.

    1. High

    2. Low

**Mental**

1. Processing – your ability to take in information and work with it intelligently

    1. High

2. Low

2. Concentrating – your ability to focus on a task and be able to maintain a high level of concentration

    1. High

    2. Low

3. Recalling – your ability to store information and remember it when necessary. Short-term and long-term memory may differ.

    1. High

2. Low

2. Based on your descriptions above, rate your highest and lowest overall level of functioning in each area in the past six months out of 10:

**Physical**

1. High ___/10

2. Low ___/10

**Emotional**

1. High ___/10

2. Low ___/10

**Mental**

1. High ___/10

2. Low ___/10

3. Within that range, identify where you are at right now in each area now as you are reading this:

1. Physical     ___/10

2. Emotional   ___/10

3. Mental      ___/10

4. Describe your awareness of functioning throughout the day. What are the assumptions you make about how you 'should' be functioning, versus where you might be at any given moment?

5. If you were to chart them on a graph at four key times – breakfast, lunch, supper and bedtime – what do you think would be times when there is a significant difference over the course of the day?

## RESPOND

1. Print off some graph paper or make a simple chart and do the exercise described in Question 5 - chart your changes in resources at four key times – breakfast, lunch, supper and bedtime throughout the week. It can be as simple as a chart rating each area out of 10 at those times.

|  | Breakfast | Lunch | Supper | Bedtime |
|---|---|---|---|---|
| Physical | /10 | /10 | /10 | /10 |
| Emotional | /10 | /10 | /10 | /10 |
| Mental | /10 | /10 | /10 | /10 |
| Spiritual | /10 | /10 | /10 | /10 |

2. Make a note this week of the changes that occur as the week progresses and describe the trend that you are noticing. Describe if or how things shift on the weekend.

# DAY 20: WHAT IS THE STRESS CYCLE?: ORIGINS

**STRESS CYCLE ORIGINS**

The development of stress makes the most sense if we think of it in terms of a cycle. Consider the following scenario. Let's say I'm at the office on a typical day, functioning at about 70% physically. I'm about to leave work to go home for the day. I get a call from the property manager of my building to say there's been a problem. As they were doing renovations they discovered a bunch of asbestos and now they are forced to seal off the building for a few days. I'm advised to collect my files as I won't be allowed back in the office until they're finished. Reluctantly I fill a box with my files, and then another call comes in. This time it's a buddy of mine who owns a warehouse. He says he's calling around to everyone to see if they know of anyone that can give them a hand at the warehouse. Apparently the main forklift broke down and they're waiting for parts to come in, but it will be a week. He's stressed out because they have to get ready for a big shipment coming in the next day.

Being the nice guy I am, I offer to help him out. "Great!" he says, "Just come in tomorrow at 8:00 – I'll let the supervisor know to expect you." I finish packing up my box of files and head out to the parkade, which is dark. With the box in front of me, I can't see where I'm going and I trip and fall. I smash my arm on the pavement and as I get up I can't bend my elbow and it's swelling fast. I go to the hospital for some X-rays, and as I fear, it's broken. They put a cast on me, but the doctor warns that I shouldn't try and lift anything for at least a week, until it has a chance to set. My physical resources have dipped. Now, instead of 70%, I'd say I'm closer to 40% - I've only got one good left arm.

The next day I go to the warehouse anyway, as I promised my buddy I would help. As I arrive, the supervisor is briefing everyone about the fact that they need the heavy crates in the aisles moved out of the way up onto the second shelf. Then they can get the lighter boxes from the first shelf shifted to the corner so they have room for the shipment coming in at noon. I am directed to start in the corner by myself. At this point I have a problem. In order for me to lift those crates blocking the aisles I would need to be at 90% of my peak capacity. However, I'm closer to 40%. That creates a gap.

## THE GAP

The gap is important here, because it creates stress. The demand is higher than my available resources. In fact, that's what I want to use as my own definition of stress: I feel stress when there is a real or perceived demand that exceeds available resources. It's a simple concept that we'll explore further. Let's get back to my story. What happens next? Well, I'm in the warehouse, feeling stress. But maybe I'm a little stubborn. I think to myself, there must be some way I can move this crate. I stoop down and pick up the corner with my good hand, prop it up with my foot, and then try to jam my good arm underneath and slide it up the side of the shelving unit. This doesn't work though – in fact, there's no way that I'm going to be able to lift an 80 pound crate above my head with one arm, by myself. It's not going to happen. In fact, I'm going to fail 100% of the time.

---

**Key Concept:** *"The gap is created by your demand compared to your current resources."*

---

Now, how do we typically feel when we fail? Right – lousy! We get down and discouraged. More negative emotions. I am also thinking to myself, "If only I was as strong and healthy as I used to be, and I didn't have this stupid broken arm. Then I could lift these crates and show these younger guys a thing or two." There's nothing wrong with that as a desire, but it clearly is not going to be met today. Now I have an unmet desire which produces more negative emotions. With all of these negative emotions dragging me down, my emotional resources will likely decrease as well. Now I have even fewer resources to use going forward, the gap increases, my stress increases, and the cycle gets worse.

## "THE GAP" RECAP

So let's review this quickly:

**STRESS** – is created when there's a gap between demand and resources

**FAILURE** – I can't meet the demand, and I fail 100% of the time. I feel lousy as a result

**DESIRE** – My desire to succeed and prove myself to others fails. I feel more negative emotions

*The cycle continues and gets worse, draining my resource levels even more. This is not good!*

# DAY 20 WORKSHEET

## *REACT*

1. Describe how you think that this example is applicable to more than just warehouses.

2. Describe how you see yourself in this cycle.

3. What strikes you about this scenario in terms of your own life?

## REFLECT

1. Give an example of this type of scenario that you can recall from this past week.

2. Did you find your stress and frustration levels increasing? How did you attempt to manage this? Was it successful? Why or why not?

3. How do you feel when you fail?

4. How does that affect your self-esteem?

5. What does that do to your motivation to want to try again?




6. How do you feel when you want to give up?




**RESPOND**

1. Knowing that a gap between demands and resources produces stress, can you identify the major gaps that exist in your life right now?

    1.

    2.

    3.

2. List the ways in which you can possibly reduce the gaps that exist.

1.

2.

3.

.

3. Think of ways that you can better identify gaps before they become too significant. What are the warning signs that you could become aware of?

# DAY 21: WHAT IS THE STRESS CYCLE?: VENDING MACHINE

## THE VENDING MACHINE

Here's another way to look at this. Imagine you are thirsty, and desperate for something to drink. Up ahead you see a vending machine, and you are thrilled at the prospect of getting a refreshing can of soda pop. You see that they have your favorite drink, and it's only $1.50. You dig around in your pockets for some change. All you have, though, is a dollar. You're short 50 cents. Now, would you really put in the dollar anyway, and start pushing the button over and over and over for fifteen minutes? I'm hoping you would say "No way!" because that would be silly. You don't have enough money. In other words, you don't have sufficient resources to get that which you desire.

## ARE WE SILLY?

However, I believe that we as humans are actually kind of silly because I think we do this all the time. We don't do this with vending machines, because it's much too obvious what's going on. However, I think we do this in other areas of our life, where we can see something we want, it seems like it's right there in front of us, and we want it so badly that we keep trying to make it happen. But it doesn't and we get more and more frustrated and stressed out as a result. This happens frequently in relationships, where we want someone to do something or change something, but they don't and our frustration rises. Or we want to get more done at work, but we don't seem to have the resources to make it happen, and it drives us nuts! Clearly we need an alternative solution. The good news is there is one. Let's carry on to see what it is.

---

**Key Concept:** *"Pushing the vending machine button happens often in life. Our demand is right infront of us and we expect to get it regardless of resources."*

---

**(Refer to Appendix 2 at the end of the book for a diagram of preceding content)**

# DAY 21 WORKSHEET

## *REACT*

1. Did this example of the vending machine strike you as being silly?

2. How do you think this example can apply to anything in your life?

## *REFLECT*

1. In what ways does the idea of continuing to try to change something that we can't change ring true in your life?

2. Have you ever tried to do this in your relationships – tried to change someone and been frustrated that it didn't happen the way we wanted it to?

## RESPOND

1. If there is one thing that you could change about the way you are dealing with a situation right now, what would it be?

2. How would you implement this in your life this week? What would you do differently?

3. Are you open to exploring alternatives to this pattern?

# DAY 22: WHAT IS THE STRESS CYCLE?: DE-STRESS CYCLE

## DE-STRESS CYCLE

So we now know what creates stress: Trying and failing to meet a demand that exceeds available resources. So let's try something different. Imagine you were asked to divide a paper in half, into two columns. On the one side, the heading is THINGS I DON'T CONTROL, and on the other side THINGS I DO CONTROL. This might seem like a pretty simple way to split up your life, but trust me for a moment here. First a trick question: "On what side of the paper are we going to put desires?

You could make a case for saying the DO CONTROL side, because we choose what we desire. However, I'm going to say that we have to put desires on the DON'T CONTROL side if we use the definition from before, because we defined desires as "things that we want to have happen that we don't fully control." Ok? So let's do that. Now, we need something for the other side. We're going to use the term goals, but define it a little differently than you might be expecting. I'm going to say that goals are things we want that we do fully control – 100%.

To simplify: A goal is something I control. It even rhymes! But if it is a goal that I control, it has to be completely within my capacity. Think about that for a moment. If it's not fully within my capacity, it's not really a goal, it's a desire. And there's nothing wrong with desires, but unmet desires produce negative emotions, including stress, right? And aren't those exactly what we're trying to get rid of?!! But if I do have an actual goal, and it is within my capacity, then I have the chance for 100% success. The next question of course, is: "How do we feel when we have success?" The answer is "Great!" What happens to my emotional resources when I have success? They increase, and I feel better, plus I am better able to cope. Also, increased resources lead to increased ability to cope, which leads to lowering my stress level, which is what we have set out to accomplish!

---

**Key Concept:** *"Desires are things we want that we DON'T fully control. Goals are things we want we DO fully control - 100%!"*

---

## DE-STRESS SUMMARY

Let's summarize this De-Stress Cycle now. Recognize that desires are on the DON'T CONTROL side of our list, and that goals are things we DO CONTROL 100%. A goal is only a goal if it is entirely within our current capacity. When we have goals we have the chance for 100% success, and we feel great What makes more sense?

*Unmet desires = failure = feel crappy.*

*Goals are met = success = feel happy!*

Now that we've distinguished between desires and goals, which side of the chart does it make the most sense to live on? Which side produces more pleasant results? If you had to pick one, the choice may seem clear to you now – I think we would all choose 100% success over 100% failure! We need to translate our desires into a series of goals that we can control.

So if this is so obvious, why don't we do this? What's the missing link? We want the answer to the third question: "How can we regulate stress?"

# DAY 22 WORKSHEET

## *REACT:*

1. What is your initial reaction to the difference between desires and goals?

2. What about these seems like it wouldn't work?

3. What is your reaction to the simplicity of this model?

## *REFLECT:*

1. In what ways have you been confusing goals and desires?

2. How have these affected your relationships?




3. What other ways could clearly seeing this distinction improve your life?




## *RESPOND:*

1. What are some ways that you could identify instantly whether something is a desire or a goal?

2. Identify all of the negative emotions you've had this past week. Can you figure out which unmet desires are creating them?

Emotion #1:

Unmet Desire #1:

Emotion #2:

Unmet Desire #2:

Emotion #3:

Unmet Desire #3:

3. Now see if you can make a plan to start to translate those desires into goals – 'goalify' them

# DAY 23: REGULATING STRESS: MISSING LINK

## MISSING LINK

Okay – here's what we've been waiting for - the answer to why we allow ourselves to suffer with so much stress and so many negative emotions. Well, let's head back to the warehouse first to sort this out.

Imagine I'm in the corner of the warehouse still trying to lift those crates. I figure out that I can't lift them on my own, and head over to talk to the supervisor. I suggest that because I can't lift the crates by myself, I could have another person, that can't lift the crates alone either, come and lift the other side, so that together we could get them out of the aisles and onto the second shelf. If that doesn't work, I mention that I could always grab a clipboard and start tracking the inventory to ensure that things are going to the right spot, or perhaps grab a broom and start sweeping the place. I don't really care what I do, I just want to give 100% of what I have, I say to him.

Now the supervisor might turn and take one look at me and say, "What, you lazy, good for nothing...!" and then start to swear at me. To that, I'd shrink back, shocked at his response to my offer to help. Now, who looks like the idiot? 99% of people will say the supervisor, because of his verbally abusive reply. I would agree. But why? Because he's not willing to accept the reality of the situation. I think it is safe to say that we don't want to be idiots in life – we can let other people be idiots, but we don't want to be idiots ourselves.

But that means we have to be prepared to accept the reality of the situation in which we find ourselves, even if it isn't a reality that we particularly like or want.

## REALITY CHECK

So we know we need to accept reality? But why? Well, let's consider the alternative. I am going to fight reality instead. I'm not going to accept the way things are because I don't want them that way. I will never give up – never give in. I will prevail!!! Really? How many people have ever successfully conquered reality? The idea is laughable because we aren't powerful enough to change reality.

---

**Key Concept:** *"When facing life we have to be prepared to accept the reality of a situation, even if it's a reality we don't like or appreciate."*

---

Consider the following example…

## SAND CASTLE INCIDENT

Let's say I was at the beach by the ocean with my four year old son. We were in the middle of building an amazing sand castle, complete with turrets and high walls. It dwarfed other people's attempts to build in the sand, and my son was so excited. "Dad, this is awesome! Nothing can break it down!" my son exclaimed. I shared his enthusiasm, but was aware that the tide was starting to come in, and would soon come and destroy our amazing creation.

Trying to prepare him, I pointed out that the waves were getting closer, and he started to panic. "Dad, we have to stop them! We can't let the waves attack the castle." He started running into the water at the approaching wave, his arms outstretched and braced for impact. The wave hit him down and bowled him over with its power. He was swept under the water and struggled to the surface, gasping for air, and spitting out saltwater. Even more determined, he rushed back into the ocean to the next wave which was approaching quickly: "Dad, come help!" he cried. Although my heart wishes I could help, the bemused smile on my face indicates what I am thinking to myself: "I wish I could help you stop the waves, son, but the tide is just too strong. We have to accept it!"

We are amused at the idea that a child would try to fight the tide in order to protect his castle. For him, his desire is clear: "I want my castle to last forever!" Fighting against the waves isn't going to help the situation, though. In fact, it will just make things worse, as his disappointment will soon be coupled with frustration and exhaustion at the lack of progress he is making. We'll come back to this situation in a moment. In the meantime, let's apply the 'accepting reality' principle to the warehouse example.

# DAY 23 WORKSHEET

## *REACT*

1. What do you think of the sandcastle example?

2. What came to your mind initially as you heard the story?

## *REFLECT*

1. Do you think this example can apply to anything in your life? Why or why not?

2. Describe the areas of your life in which you may have been fighting reality recently.

1. **Work/school**

**2. Home**




**3. Finances**




**4. Other**



3. In which relationships are you trying to fight the reality that exists – pretending that things are a certain way, when they're really not?

## RESPOND

1. Make a list of the 'reality fighting situations' in your life right now.

    1.

    2.

    3.

2. Rate the stress that you feel that is a direct result of each of these situations.

    1.

    2.

    3.

# DAY 24: REGULATING STRESS: STRESS NEUTRALIZER

**LIMITATION QUESTION**

In the warehouse, my boss is being an idiot by not accepting reality. I, too, have to accept the reality of the limitations of my resources, but I can't do that without knowing what my limitations are. This brings us to the next question: "Why is it hard to figure out what my limitations are?" Well, I don't think that is a difficult question to consider. After all, don't we know automatically what we can do and what we can't? Not really. Why? Let's refer to both psychology and ancient wisdom literature to figure that out.

As both of us used to teach psychology at university, perhaps it is appropriate to make fun of ourselves and our colleagues as we provide an examples of what is referred to as 'over-confidence.' Simply defined, overconfidence is the tendency that we have as humans to overestimate the skills, abilities, control or influence we have over our life. Young or old, educated or not, we all seem to be susceptible to overconfidence. Studies have demonstrated that 94 percent of college professors think they do above average work. Similarly, 93 percent of the U.S. students estimated themselves to be "above average" drivers. Obviously, only 50 percent of people can ever be above average, by definition. Clearly, people don't typically do a good job of figuring out accurately where their limitations are.

**OVERCONFIDENCE/PRIDE**

Overconfidence in our knowledge can have hilarious results

when predictions are made about the future. Consider these gems from the 20th century:

1. "A rocket will never be able to leave the Earth's atmosphere." — New York Times, 1936.

2. "There will never be a bigger plane built." — A Boeing engineer, after the first flight of the 247, a twin engine plane that holds ten people

3. "There is no reason anyone would want a computer in their home." — Ken Olson, president, chairman and founder of Digital Equipment Corp. (DEC), maker of big business mainframe computers, arguing against the PC in 1977.

Overconfidence can also be costly. Hans Blix, the official in charge of weapons inspections in Iraq prior to the 2nd Iraq War of 2003, stated: "The governments that launched the war claimed to be 100% convinced that there were such weapons, but they had 0% knowledge of where these weapons were." 10 years later, the cost of the war was estimated to have been 1.7 trillion dollars, with another 7 trillion to eventually be paid in interest. Almost 200,000 people died in direct war deaths. 0 weapons of mass destruction were found.

In another example that has come to epitomize the dangers of overconfidence and pride, the story of the 'unsinkable' Titanic sinking on its maiden voyage is perhaps the most memorable and graphic illustration of this. An ancient proverb from the Bible states this idea simply: "Pride precedes a disaster, and an arrogant attitude precedes a fall." Proverbs 16:18 (GW). So what is the antidote?

## THE NEUTRALIZER

What can neutralize overconfidence and pride, and prevent the dangers they represent? I am going to argue that the willingness to acknowledge the limitations of our resources is required, an acknowledgment that we aren't functioning at the level we'd like to be. That willingness to acknowledge the limitations of our resources is what I call humility. And we, as humans, pretty much suck at humility. I mean, it goes against everything we're taught from the minute that we're born. We're not very good at humility in our society. We don't watch TV shows and movies that extol the virtues of humility. We don't have teachers and supervisors spending time telling us about the benefits of humility. In fact, we may not even really understand what it is.

---

**Key Concept:** *"Acknowleding our limitations while reducing pride and overconfidence can help us neutralize stress."*

---

But think of it. The only way to stress is created is when there is a gap between demands and our available resources. If we don't want stress (and the other negative emotions which typically accompany it!) we need to close the gap. If we know the limitations of our resources, we will know how to NOT exceed them. But acknowledging our limitations DEMANDS that we walk in humility. That's the tough part. So what's holding us back?

# DAY 24 WORKSHEET

## REACT

1. What is your initial reaction to this definition of humility?

2. Does the idea of humility being linked to stress make sense? Why or why not?

## REFLECT

1. What part of you resists the idea of humility?

2. What has been your understanding of humility prior to this?

3. Why is the idea of humility so foreign in our North American culture?

4. What is the biggest thing keeping us from embracing this idea?

5. When is the last time you have been willing to embrace your own limitations?

## RESPOND

1. Make an honest assessment of the limitations that you have in the four main areas of your life:

**Physical**

**Emotional**

**Mental**

**Spiritual**

2. Write down your fears in terms of accepting these realities. How would your life change if you were willing to really acknowledge them?

# DAY 25: REGULATING STRESS: MOUNTAIN CLIMBER

## SO WHY NOT ADMIT?

Let's stop and think about things for a second. We don't want to admit that we can't or aren't functioning at a level that we'd like to. Why? Well, in part because of pressure from the outside. We don't want others to become aware of the fact that we can't do the things that we're 'supposed to be able to do.' We want to give others the impression that we're as competent as we always have been, regardless of whether our resources levels have been depleted to a point that we can't complete the task at hand. We rely on the opinion of others to provide us our sense of self. Knowing that others might find out that we aren't the person we make ourselves out to be is a scary thought.

The pressure can also come from the inside. We gauge our sense of self by believing that we have always been the person that others can rely on. We define ourselves by being the 'go-to' person at work or at home. Our self-concept depends on having a constant ability to perform at a high level. We don't want to be like the 'others' – those that can't be relied on in a pressure situation. We like seeing ourselves a certain way, and humbling ourselves to accept that we may not have the resources we're used to having is not something we're prepared to accept.

It's not actually a good idea to have our sense of self be dependent on whether or not we meet the demands that are being placed on us by others or ourselves. However, if we don't have an independent way to generate a positive sense of self that doesn't rely on our level of functioning, then we are stuck. But what is keeping us stuck? What is the one thing that will prevent us from embracing the idea of humility? It's really a three letter word, that begins with E. If you can't think of it immediately, let me reveal the source of all of our trouble. Our EGO! Our ego is actually the thing that gets in the way of us being able to walk in humility through life. So why can't we let go of our ego? Let's try and answer that question...

## EGO ON THE MOUNTAIN

Because I like telling stories, and this one will illustrate our point nicely, here's a scenario for you. I am climbing a mountain, and I eventually reach the top. I'm wearing a bright orange parka, and am visible to the hikers below. They see me at the top, and even though they're too far away to clearly see, they are cheering at my accomplishment. They are impressed by what an incredible mountain climber I am. I relish the thought that they obviously think I'm awesome. I attempt to take a selfie so I can post it and let my friends at home know that I've made it and that I am amazing. As I'm moving close to the edge of the cliff to get a better shot, the snow shifts, and the ice shelf starts breaking away. I desperately grab for the rope and finally get a good grip when I'm over the edge. I swing back into the cliff wall, dislocating my shoulder in the process. I don't have the strength to climb back up to safety, but

I don't want to let go either. I'm not sure that I will have a safe landing in the snow below or if there are rocks that will kill me if fall. I am stuck in a precarious position – I am not the hiker that the people below think I am, and even though I know I can't stay in my dangerous position forever, I don't want to let go either until I am assured that things will turn out okay if I fall.

It is tough admitting that we made a stupid mistake, or that life's situation has changed and that we aren't functioning the way that others think we should be. I believe, however, that it is necessary. Otherwise, we will always find ourselves in difficult positions because we're not willing to acknowledge that we need help, and it may end up in disaster in the end. Humility is the key that will ultimately save us. Sending up a flare to alert others to our difficult position might save the day, and may well be embarrassing, but it's our only sane option!

# DAY 25 WORKSHEET

## REACT

1. What did you think about the hiker example? Have you ever felt like this before?

## REFLECT

1. Why does our ego resist accepting humility?

2. Do you agree that we tend to rely on other's opinions of us? How does social media influence this?

4. What have you done in the past to try and avoid relying on other's opinions to feed your ego?  Did it work?

RESPOND

1. Write down in your journal the ways in which your ego is raising your level of stress in your life.

# DAY 26: REGULATING STRESS: HOT SHOWER
## HOT SHOWER

Humility is so counter-cultural that you might be thinking to yourself, what on earth are they talking about? But here's the thing, if you want to live your life differently than the stress-filled one this culture has handed you, you are going to have to embrace concepts that are radically different than what your surroundings teach. So let's dig deeper into understanding the power humility has, because it really can neutralize excess stress in our lives. To do this, I want you to imagine being a friend's house where you are staying for the weekend. They have an older place that has been restored beautifully, with original hardwood and trim that looks amazing. However, they haven't had the money to redo all of the plumbing yet. You are up early in the morning having a shower, washing your hair and enjoying the pleasantly hot water. All of a sudden you are aware of the pain as that wonderful water suddenly becomes scalding hot. You frantically try and turn off the hot water tap as you realize that someone in the other washroom has flushed the toilet, diverting the flow of cold water from your shower to refill the tank. Your friend warned you this might happen, but it doesn't mean that it hurts any less in the meantime!

Now, why is it that homes built today don't have this problem? Some brilliant person designed a valve that controls the flow of hot and cold water as they are mixed together, equalizing the pressure and temperature so that the 'hot water surprise shower' can't happen. So we know that both hot and cold water are necessary in order to have an enjoyable shower. We just want to be able to adjust the flow so that we always have a pleasant temperature.

## STRESS REGULATOR

Let's turn our attention back to managing our emotional life. Based on what we just talked about with stress, we know there are two components that determine the amount of stress that we experience on an ongoing basis: demands and resources. Think of these as our hot and cold taps, respectively. When demands (or the hot water) exceed available resources (the cold water) we immediately experience stress. But we don't like it when things get too stressful in our life – it becomes unpleasant or even dangerous. It's not good when our shower is too hot! We need to have a 'stress regulator' that can always adjust the stress that we feel in our life to a manageable level.

Imagine that demands are like the hot water in the shower. Desires can become demands that we or others place on us. To imagine that we will never have desires or demands in our lives is crazy – we have them every day and we need them to function and to provide us motivation and move us forward. We also know that we need resources to balance out the demands. Let's think of resources as the cold water. We all have some resources, even if our 'cold water flow' (resources) may be reduced due to circumstances beyond our control. What is the regulator that can regulate the proper flow of desires and demands in our lives? How can we properly balance out these opposing forces in our lives?

---

**Key Concept:** *"When demands exceed available resources we immediately experience stress"*

---

## HUMILITY

Luckily, we've already talked about this magic stress regulator, even though you may not have seen it for what it is. It is simple, yet powerful. It is easy to access, yet difficult to embrace. I'm talking, of course, about humility. It is the lever we can use to turn down the hot water flow (demands) when the cold water is limited (resources). Humility is the one thing that allows us to acknowledge how our resources might be limited right now. Then we can clearly see whether we have what we need to meet any given demand that we or others might be placing on us.

It is the gap between resources and demands that creates stress and other negative emotions and makes us feel lousy. And we can only truly see the gap through the lens of humility. When we are able to stay operating within our capacity through the awareness that comes through humility, then we don't ever have to have the experience of being 'stressed out' ever again. Either something is fully within our control, or it isn't. Either we do what we can with the resources we have and feel at peace, or we attempt to control things we can't and get stressed out.

There's only one way to reduce or eliminate stress. Adjust the demand that we allow to be placed on us so that it fits the resources we have accessible to us. There is no other way.

**(Refer to Appendix 3 at the end of the book for a diagram of preceding content)**

# DAY 26 WORKSHEET

## *REACT*

1. Do you think the shower idea is too simplistic? Why or why not?

2. What is your reaction to the phrase "The gap makes us feel like crap!"?

## *REFLECT*

1. Describe what having no demands (and no stress!) whatsoever would be like. Would it be unpleasant – like a cold shower?

2. What is your stress level – the 'temperature in your shower' right now?

3. In what ways do you feel like you are 'raising the temperature' without knowing it?




4. Describe how this model's focus on our own responsibility for our stress level affects you. Does this provide a relief to you or increase your stress?




5. What are the top five stressors on your mind today?

    1.

    2.

3.


4.


5.



6. What are the ways that you feel you could start to regulate your own stress level?

1.

2.

3.

4.

5.

## RESPOND

1. Write down in your journal the things you could do right now that would help to decrease your own stress level.

2. Choose one of these things and implement it in your life... today! Then call a close friend or family member and tell them what you did.

# DAY 27: HOW CAN WE REGULATE OUR STRESS?: THE UTILITY OF HUMILITY

## HOW DOES THIS WORK?

Let's go back to the story of Tasha. Here it is again in case you can't remember that far back. See if you can identify the 'gaps' that exist in her life that are causing her stress – we'll review them after.

## STORY OF TASHA

Tasha is just about to leave work to go home when her boss walks by her, and causally drops a file on her desk. "Make sure this is done by 8:00 am tomorrow – the client is coming by the office to review it at 8:30." Tasha instantly realizes her carefully laid plans to celebrate her daughter's birthday this evening with her family would have to change, or she would risk disappointing her boss. She also feels a knot in the pit of her stomach as she realizes the painful conversation that will involve her husband and kids as they realize they won't be able to go out as planned. She feels her heart rate rise and senses her breathing rate increasing. As she collects her papers and the file and walks to the car she realizes that she forgot her phone inside her office along with her keys. Her frustration mounts as she bangs on the door to get back into the office, but the receptionist has already left for the day. She can't get a hold of her family to let them know that not only will she not be able to meet them at the restaurant for supper, but that she will be late getting back now too. She feels her stress level rising inside of her and she pulls a cigarette out of her purse and lights it up. Her muscles tighten in her neck as she strains to see if anyone else is coming out of the office. Slowly she slumps down against the front door and a tear comes to her eye. Most people might say that Tasha is now officially stressed!

## GAP GLASSES

Now let's take a look at the story through 'gap glasses' – those seeing aids that allow us to identify gaps between demands and resources. The first gap is between the time resources Tasha has, and the demand of the boss to have the file ready by morning. The resultant emotion is a feeling of pressure. The second gap exists in the space between family expectations of a birthday celebration, and the conflict with workplace demands. The likely negative emotion is fear of disappointing her family. The next gap exists between the time demand she has on her and her phone and keys being stuck for an indefinite period in the office. She feels frustrated as a result.

## CLOSING THE GAP

Now the next task begins – how to turn down the 'hot water' and close these gaps, using humility. Gap 1 forces Tasha to evaluate her resources. She has made an assumption about the amount of time it will take her to prepare the file for the client the next day – and she believes that it won't allow her to spend the evening with her family. Is that assumption true, however? As she waits outside for someone to let her back into the office building, Tasha could recognize this perceived demand, and seek to verify its accuracy

– see if it's valid, in other words. While she faces the entrance, she flips through the paperwork, noting those parts which are still incomplete. She assesses that the missing sections will take a couple of hours to finish, but then remembers that her colleague hasn't submitted a significant part of the report, yet. Mentally, she makes a note to email the colleague, and request that it be printed out first thing the next day and given to the secretary to add to the file before 8:30.

---

**Key Concept:** *"'Gap Glasses' allow us to identify gaps between demands and resources."*

---

# DAY 27 WORKSHEET

## REACT

1. What is your initial reaction to the Tasha story and how things worked out?

## REFLECT

1. Describe a time when you were able to find a way to do what Tasha did – find a way to navigate a crisis in an unexpected way.

2. What are your thoughts about the idea of 'gap glasses.'

3. What was the last situation in which you could have really used some 'gap glasses?'

4. What are your thoughts about the value of increasing your awareness of the gap as a means to start to address it?

## RESPOND

1. Keep track of the gaps in your life and review them at the end of the day. See how much easier it is to identify them when you are looking for them.

# DAY 28 HOW CAN WE REGULATE OUR STRESS?: THE DASHBOARD OF LIFE

**THE DASHBOARD**

A dashboard in a car has lights that come on at specific times when there is a part of the car requires attention. Seeing the "Low oil" or "Check engine" signs lit up would normally prompt a call to action. Pulling into a mechanic to get things attended to may be the next step. The light itself simply alerts the driver to something needing to be addressed under the hood.

Perhaps we can think of negative emotions in a similar way. Maybe they are simply an indication to us of a gap that needs to be addressed in one of two ways – either increase resources (seek out additional support in humility) or decrease demand (change the expectation we have of ourselves in that situation in order adjust to the reality that exists). Again, this may seem too simplistic. "Surely not every negative emotion is caused by an unmet desire!" you might think. Well, let's examine a few situations more closely to see if the "dashboard light" theory could be true.

**MORNING**

Let's start on a typical day. The alarm goes off beside my head. I'm tired and hit the snooze button, craving a few more minutes of sleep. I drift off into a peaceful slumber until nine minutes later when my alarm goes off again. I know that I should really get up, but my desire to experience a blissful state prompts me to hit the alarm a second time. When I finally get up the next time the alarm blares, I'm now 18 minutes late in terms of my regular schedule.

There is officially a gap between the time I have (resources) and the demands on me (work out, shower, get dressed and ready, eat breakfast, etc.) I start feeling pressure and stress knowing I have to leave early this morning to get to a meeting at work. The light on the 'dashboard of life' has come on.

I feel 'stressed out,' which is a negative emotion. My next step is to recognize that the emotion is an indication that there is a gap. I have to identify the unmet desire associated with the negative emotion: "I want to get to work on time but still maintain my usual routine." That is a great desire, but a lousy goal; I can't control time! Now, it was my choice to keep hitting the snooze button and I shouldn't be surprised that I am in this position. Nevertheless, I can close the gap by using humility. Recognizing that it is not possible to make more time (resources are limited), I can instead, decrease the demand on myself to carry out my routine in the normal way. I can instantly adjust my expectations to reflect the new reality, and make a choice to 'save' 20 minutes by not working out. Or, maybe I decide to work out, but don't shower (I now have another issue – how to avoid embarrassment from stinking at work!). Perhaps I don't eat breakfast as a way of saving time. There are all sorts of ways that I can close the gap that exists in my life in this area. It's when I don't walk in humility and stubbornly refuse to accept the reality that exists that my stress and other negative emotions increase and intensify.

**WORK**

Maybe I arrive at work, on time, but am faced with a situation similar to Tasha – my boss puts some paperwork on my desk and says "I need this done by noon." I feel panic or stress again (the negative emotion). I track it back to my unmet desire: "I want to please my boss and get this assignment done by lunch." Great desire? Yes, but a lousy goal. Identifying the gap is simple: my perception that I have to get it done, and the reality that exists in terms of the limited time frame. Humility can help us here, too. I need to translate my desire into goals I can control, so I start by assessing the situation. Maybe I double-check to make sure that the paperwork will, in fact, take the expected time to complete. Next, I examine the reality of my track record in the past in terms of completing that assignment. If it has always taken me six hours to process the paperwork, and my boss has just suggested I complete it before noon (four hours away), then clearly I will be a stressed out mess the entire morning if I attempt to achieve what is almost certainly impossible. Admitting that I can't get the task done by lunch may be difficult if I'm not used to walking in humility, but it is essential unless I want to start experiencing stress symptoms immediately.

Closing the gap means that I will have to have a conversation with my boss, and admit to them that I have never completed paperwork in less than six hours previously, but that I am willing to do my best to see how much I can get done. Then, I could suggest a couple of options, including having a co-worker complete part of it if it really needs to be done by noon. Alternatively, I might see if there is a way to postpone the deadline itself so it isn't creating unnecessary stress on me and decreasing my performance, or increasing the likelihood of mistakes that will be made if I rush through it.

---

**Key Concept:** *"Humility is essential if we want to avoid being stressed out."*

---

Clearly attempting to do the impossible has a small chance of success. Attempting to try anyway is not only silly, but stress-inducing. Calmly assessing the reality that exists and planning for a way to move through it that allows me to stay regulated emotionally is a better alternative.

# DAY 28 WORKSHEET

## REACT

1. What is your initial reaction to the idea of the 'dashboard of life?'

## REFLECT

1. Do you think that the function of negative emotions is simply to identify gaps? What other purposes do you think that they serve?

2. Describe a time when you used negative emotions to identify something important in your life that was 'out of alignment.'

3. Describe how taking a step back from your negative emotions could be beneficial in determining the next steps you could take to make your situation better.

4. When was the last time that disengaging from your negative emotion long enough to analyze what was really going on would have been beneficial for you or a relationship?

**RESPOND**

1. Keep track of the times when your 'dashboard' lights up. See if you can quickly start utilizing that as a signal to take a positive step to address the situation.

# DAY 29: SUMMARY + NEXT STEPS

## SUMMARY

So, what have we learned? We started with the problem that we all experience: stress. You have been reading this far because you don't want to be as stressed as you are, and you want relief. You probably wanted a simple, effective solution that was guaranteed to work 100% of the time. That, we believe, is what you now have. You now understand how to identify stress in your life and its symptoms in a variety of areas – physical, emotional, mental, behavioral. You have a better understanding of stress and the mechanisms by which stress is produced and maintained. You also now know a guaranteed strategy of reducing stress – should you be willing to embrace it.

## STRANDED HIKERS?

For those who feel like they are in a precarious position and that they can't bring themselves to let go of their false sense of self, like the hiker on the mountain, we understand. It's a difficult thing to do. You may need to explore other options for your sense of self to be maintained that don't involve attempting to over-function and failing. For you, we recommend our course, "The Simple Self-Esteem Solution", which guarantees a pathway for you to develop and maintain a positive self-esteem every day, regardless of your resource levels, and regardless of what's going on around you in your life. It works whether people think you're amazing, or whether they are always upset with you. It works regardless of your failures of the past, or your fear of the future. It recognizes the role that others play in how you feel about yourself, but allows you to move forward in freedom as you become strong, confident and secure in who you are. If that sounds appealing, go to our website to find out more.

---

**Key Concept:** *"Having the knowledge about emotions and the mechanisms of stress will allow you to reduce the negative effects of stress."*

---

## BOUNDARY ISSUES?

For others of you who have no problem in walking in humility, step into your future and get ready to enjoy a whole new world of stress-free living. Emotional Freedom begins with embracing humility, and accepting reality. If you feel like the difficulty might be in communicating your limitations to others, because they won't be willing to accept that you can't do what they are demanding, we understand. Setting and maintaining boundaries, and standing up to those who don't seem to take "No" for an answer is difficult. If you're used to pleasing other people then walking in humility might be tough. We want to assist you in that as well.

Going through this workbook is a good start, but what will be especially beneficial to you are courses and seminars we offer on Relational Freedom, which describes a way to communicate effectively where you're at and create opportunities to be heard, understood, and validated. Visit www.thestresscenter.ca if you are interested in current information about these.

# DAY 29 WORKSHEET

## *REACT*

1. Do you feel like the questions that were posed initially were answered sufficiently? Why or why not?




## *REFLECT*

1. How has your ability to identify stress changed after going through this workbook?







2. How has your ability to understand stress changed after going through this workbook?

3. How has your ability to reduce your stress changed after going through this workbook?

## RESPOND

1. In your journal, write down the things you would like to know more about to assist you in being better able at identifying your stress.

2. In your journal, write down the things you would like to know more about to assist you in being better able at understanding your stress.

3. In your journal, write down the things you would like to know more about to assist you in being better able at reducing your stress.

4. Send your responses to info@thestresscenter.ca, so that we can give some more information and connect you with others in your

journey to regulate your stress!

# DAY 30: WHAT NOW? JOIN US!
## WHAT ABOUT NOW?

For those who say – "You don't understand! Realizing that my rent is due, and I don't have enough money to pay it, doesn't reduce my stress. It's still there!" Our point is this. You might not be able to change your reality immediately the way you want to. Your desire is to have enough money for rent. We get it. But here's a simple question: "Is getting stressed out about this going to help?" Is not sleeping, getting sick, missing work and being miserable going to be beneficial to solve your problem? Is being on edge and becoming irritable with your family going to bring you closer together or divide you and make things worse?

---

**Key Concept:** *"Assessing your situation, applying humility and understanding that being stressed will not help you, will reduce negative emotions."*

---

If you are walking in humility, and realize that you are short of money because of poor financial decisions you have made is the problem, then you are more likely to seek assistance to help you with that – calling a debt consolidation company may be the first step within your control. Maybe you have parents that could assist you with making rent payments, but you're too proud to ask them for the money. Humility will help you with making that call and accessing their assistance. Maybe if this is a one-time event, and you've been a model tenant in other respects, your landlord will be willing to give you more time until you can figure a way to get the money together. Humbling yourself and talking to them may be the first step in moving toward a temporary, and then a more permanent, solution. Maybe realizing that you don't really have the income to afford to live in the place you are right now will be an important step toward finding a more suitable accommodation that may be smaller or further away from work or school, but which may allow you to reduce your stress every month because you know that you can pay the rent.

In all the cases mentioned above, being stressed out isn't going to help you think more clearly and set goals within your limitations. It's just going to make things worse. That's why you need to de-stress yourself first, so you can move to the next step, which involves using your resources effectively to better address the problem.

We want to be there to help you along the way. And there are others like you that will have ideas that you may never have even thought about that will assist you in your current situation. By completing this workbook you have gained access to the Stress Center community – a group of individuals who are seeking to gain increasing levels of freedom in all areas of their lives – emotional, personal, and relational. They may be the biggest resource of all that can help you as you reduce your stress, one step at time. Go to **www.thestresscenter.ca** now to register now.

In the meantime, check out our blog and twitter feed for more tips on how to de-stress yourself. Remember, humility is the key to freedom!

## EXECUTIVE SUMMARY

There are external stressors all around us. Our experience of stress, however, comes when we fight reality and attempt to control the things we can't. The quickest and best solution is to walk in humility by doing what we can with the resources we have, and start translating our desires into goals we fully control. This will result in success and help expand our capacity, moving us closer to having our desires met by closing the gaps in our lives.

**Therefore, to de-stress ourselves we need to:**

*1. Embrace humility*

*2. Accept reality*

*3. Expand capacity*

### JOIN US TODAY!
*www.facebook.com/thestresscenter/*

# DAY 30 WORKSHEET

## *REACT*

1. What is your reaction to the idea that humility can always help us?

## *REFLECT*

1. Describe a past situation in your life in which humility has helped you.

2. Describe a current situation in which you feel like humility may be helpful.

3. In what way will joining the Stress Center community be beneficial?

## RESPOND:

1. Go to on the following link to the Stress Center Facebook page **(www.facebook.com/thestresscenter/)** to become a member of the community that is there to support you as you transition to a life with less stress!

# APPENDIX 1

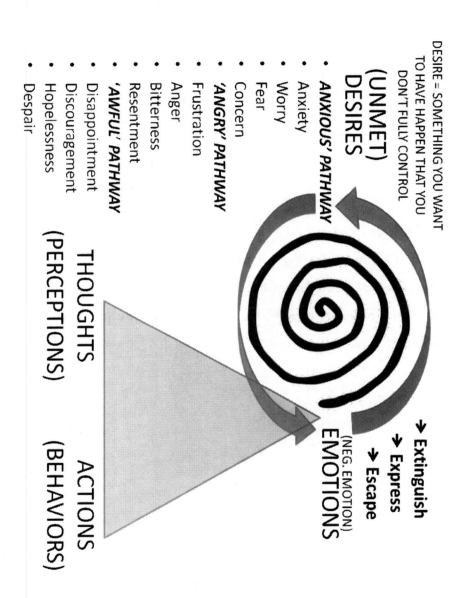

DESIRE = SOMETHING YOU WANT TO HAVE HAPPEN THAT YOU DON'T FULLY CONTROL

**(UNMET) DESIRES**

- ***ANXIOUS' PATHWAY***
  - Anxiety
  - Worry
  - Fear
  - Concern
- ***ANGRY' PATHWAY***
  - Frustration
  - Anger
  - Bitterness
  - Resentment
- ***AWFUL' PATHWAY***
  - Disappointment
  - Discouragement
  - Hopelessness
  - Despair

THOUGHTS (PERCEPTIONS)

ACTIONS (BEHAVIORS)

EMOTIONS (NEG. EMOTION)

→ Extinguish
→ Express
→ Escape

# APPENDIX 2

PHYSICAL
- 100%
- 90% UNMET DESIRE
- 70%
- 35% STRESS
- 2% 100% FAILURE

EMOTIONAL
- 70%

MENTAL

SPIRITUAL

STRESS = A REAL OR PERCEIVED DEMAND THAT EXCEEDS AVAILABLE RESOURCES
100% FAILURE = NEGATIVE EMOTIONAL STATES
UNMET DESIRE = NEGATIVE EMOTIONAL STATES

# APPENDIX 3

## WHAT IS THE ALTERNATIVE?

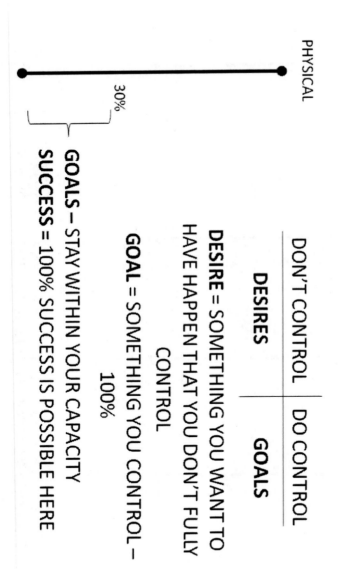

| DON'T CONTROL | DO CONTROL |
|---|---|
| DESIRES | GOALS |

**DESIRE** = SOMETHING YOU WANT TO HAVE HAPPEN THAT YOU DON'T FULLY CONTROL

**GOAL** = SOMETHING YOU CONTROL – 100%

**GOALS** – STAY WITHIN YOUR CAPACITY
**SUCCESS** = 100% SUCCESS IS POSSIBLE HERE

PHYSICAL

30%

CPSIA information can be obtained
at www.ICGtesting.com
Printed in the USA
LVOW10s0539200318
570432LV00004B/9/P